"This book focuses on what leaders can do to make tangible improvements to people's wellbeing and increase performance at the same time. It's a 'must read' for any leader who wants to make a real difference in the modern workplace."

Rachel Suff, Senior Policy Adviser (Employment Relations), Chartered Institute of Personnel and Development (CIPD)

"In a world where the importance of doing business responsibly is increasingly apparent to consumers and employees, Natasha has captured what responsible leaders should be considering to take better care of their people, as well as themselves. A contemporary leadership skill set requires humility alongside the ability to inspire, give direction and engage at all levels. This book makes it clear what steps leaders can take and how that can lead to higher levels of performance and wellbeing in their teams."

Gareth Powell, Chief Operating Officer

"The pressures of modern working life are taking an increasing toll on our physical and mental health. This carefully researched book provides a practical guide to how we can take better care of ourselves and others and not survive but thrive at work and at home too."

Simon Heath, Managing Director, Speech Bubble EQ

Published by
LID Publishing Limited
The Record Hall, Studio 204,
16-16a Baldwins Gardens,
London EC1N 7RJ, UK

524 Broadway, 11th Floor, Suite 08-120,
New York, NY 10012, US

info@lidpublishing.com
www.lidpublishing.com

A member of:

www.businesspublishersroundtable.com

Printed in Great Britain by TJ International
ISBN: 978-1-912555-07-9

Cover and page design: Matthew Renaudin

Natasha Wallace

THE
CONSCIOUS
EFFECT

**50 Lessons for Better
Organizational Wellbeing**

MADRID | MEXICO CITY | LONDON
NEW YORK | BUENOS AIRES
BOGOTA | SHANGHAI | NEW DELHI

CONTENTS

ACKNOWLEDGMENTS

Based on a few challenging experiences I've faced over recent years, I had started to lose faith in humanity. If writing this book did nothing else, it restored my faith. The tremendous kindness and effort that people have made to help me has been overwhelming and I have been truly humbled by the wonderful people I am surrounded by.

There are an endless number of people I have to thank. Not just for helping me with this book, but for helping me along my journey of consciousness and personal growth.

Firstly, to my mum. The most inspirational woman in my life. She gave me the self belief to know that I could achieve anything. She also taught me that diversity, in people and ideas, is one of the wonders of life. You are truly a woman of the world, and I hope I grow up to be as wise as you one day.

To my beautiful girls. You truly nourish me and when times are tough, you keep me in balance. Thank you for all of your smiles, your cuddles, your wise words, your hilarious antics and your curiosity. I have a lot to learn from you. I hope to be able to guide you to achieve the balance and happiness that you deserve.

To Miller. Thank you for staying on the book-writing rollercoaster with me. For all of cherub entertainment you provided, for all of the dinners you cooked, for all of the tea you made, and for being there for me through thick and thin. Thank you for recognizing when I push myself too hard (I'm still learning) and for tolerating my endless stream of consciousness. And thank you for being the sort of leader I want to be.

To my sisters, Silkie and Sapphire. Two remarkable women who are strong, dedicated, wise and loyal. Thank you for making me the proudest eldest sister. For being there when

I thought I was losing my mind. For loving me no matter how much I mess up. And for making me laugh more than anyone else ever can (except for mum, of course).

To my 'ray of sunshine' friend, Laura Sparks. You have helped me in so many ways. You've shown me the importance of friendship, self care, motherhood, laughter, tears and cuddles. You've cared for my children as if they were your own and have given me so many words of encouragement, I could fill a book with them. Thank you for your unconditional love. It means so much.

To Simon Heath, an amazing mentor and illustrator. You've challenged me and have been so incredibly generous with your time and your wisdom. You embody so much of what this book is about. You care, you bring people together, you are humble, you see the good in others, and you are dedicated to making the world of work a better place. Big love to my first-ever proper mentor. You rock.

To Gareth Powell, who showed me that you can lead tons of people and still be a genuinely good, kind and calm leader. You inspire me in so many ways. Through your curiosity, through your own commitment to personal growth, through your total dedication to making the workplace a great place to be – and for never forgetting what matters most – family.

To Neil and Kate Usher, a dream team who have helped me in so many ways. Thank you, Neil, for keeping me sane as I navigated my way through the bonkers world of book writing as a first-time writer. And to Kate, for being a woman who is such an important and positive supporter of other women. If it wasn't for you, I may have strayed through my mid-life in a straight jacket.

To Stuart Hearn, for trusting me to do something new with his team. Stuart has a different idea of what the workplace should look like and thoroughly believes in the amazing potential of others. You are the embodiment of an 'enabling leader' and could teach the world a lot about what it means to be a leader. You are a true inspiration.

To Siwan Rees, for being a powerhouse of a woman who kept me going in the early days of the new business, introducing me to my business soulmate Kate Millington-Lusardi. Without you, Kate, there would be no book. You saved me from the referencing black hole and your endless positivity kept me smiling. Both of you are going to make a big and positive difference to the world, and I am so glad to have you in my life.

To Jeremy Dean for opening my eyes to the world of riders and elephants and for showing me that when you put your mind to it, you can achieve anything. Your endless positively, creativity and willingness to iterate gave me a new understanding for how to tackle my work. And now we get to improve the world of work together.

To Sean Ruane, who introduced me to the concept of 'real talk' and how to have difficult conversations. For your endless enthusiasm, dedication to self improvement, and for the remarkable way you've bounced back from adversity to go on to help others in such a powerful way. You are a 'bright spot' in our world and we are lucky to have you.

To David Beeney for helping me to carry my children in the dead of night over rough festival terrain. Who knew our first encounter would lead to such a wonderful and blossoming relationship? Knowing there are people like you making such a positive difference to mental health gives me huge amounts of hope. So honoured to be with you on this mission.

To Vikki Perkins and Julian Baker for making my time in Cardiff so awesome. For the giggles, the 'real talk', the comradery and the friendship. As the 'Welsh Musketeers', we're going to make the world of work a better place. Fact.

To Judith Lowe and Ben Grassby, who caught me before I fell off the cliff. You taught me so much about 'self' and helped me to rediscover who I really am. You were at the beginning of my journey of consciousness and played such an incredibly important part in my awakening and new found strength. Thank you.

To Paula Leach for her heady combination of tenacity and compassion and for giving me the kick I needed to start writing this book. I always told myself that I would never be a hardnosed power-crazed HR Director. You showed me that you can combine a focus on performance with caring for people. You are truly an inspiration to womankind.

Thank you to Luke Thomas from Spring, who helped me get my head in to 'project business set up' in the early days.

To Racheal Wheatley from Watertight Marketing, who convinced me that just because you've started down a certain path doesn't mean you have to follow it.

To Bernie from Innovative Enterprise, who reassured me that out of adversity can come opportunity and the ability to help so many others. You're doing amazing work.

To Hilary Scarlett from Scarlett and Grey, who helped me get my head around neuroscience and what is really going on in the complex world of brain.

To Gethin Nadin from Benefex, who made me question my financial habits and taught me about the realities of financial stress. Thank you for also being a pioneer of workplace wellbeing; we need more of you in our world.

To Perry Timms for making me think. For making it OK to challenge how we've been doing HR for so long and to do it with such grace and kindness. You're the killer combo – provocateur and carer.

To Gary Gill, for letting me come on board with the Engage for Success movement and for giving me the opportunity to bring together an amazing group of passionate people all wanting to improve the workplace.

To Orla Power from LHH Penna, for spending hours tirelessly pouring over leadership programme design and for bringing so much energy and knowledge to our programmes. I started my leadership development journey with you. I wouldn't be here now without you.

To Matt Brooks from MBHRN, for figuring out my first business name over a bottle of wine. I came to you for a job and you convinced me to go it alone. I definitely wouldn't be here without you (and the wine).

To Jonathan Walker, my first-ever coachee as a self-employed coach. You made my personal coaching journey so enjoyable through your open-mindedness and commitment to personal growth.

To Dan Anticich, for reminding me about my spiritual side, that we have to think beyond ourselves, and that all we really need is love.

To Lesley Swarbrick, for making me feel normal. You are a remarkable HR Director with the insight and wisdom to change minds. Who knows what the future holds, but there's an exciting project bubbling there for us somewhere.

For Brenda B. Jones from the NTL Institute, who gave me the space to explore my deep hidden self and arrive at discoveries that I didn't think possible. You led me to remove the sugar coating to see what was really going on. A tough and powerful turning point in my life. Thank you.

To Antony Slumbers, for teaching me about space and the future of work. Between you and Paula Leach, you opened my eyes to the important interface between humans and tech, tearing me out of my Luddite ways and dragging me kicking and screaming into the 21st century.

To Alex Jeffers from Glue Digital Studio, for saving me from website death. I've learned a lot on my business owner journey and I know I will never be a website developer, so thank goodness we have people like you in the world to look after us.

To everyone at Tramshed Tech in Cardiff, who showed me that there was a different and better way to work. A workspace full of diverse people with diverse ideas, all with the passion to help each other. In particular to Guy Porteous, who's constant positivity and ability to bring people together made my first few weeks alone a lot less scary.

To Peter Wakefield from Loving Monday, who helped me remember what emotions were and the importance of them in the workplace. It's amazing that I ever really forgot about them really.

To Simon Michaels from Mindful Work, who is the living embodiment of why we should all be practising mindful mediation. You are the most zen businessperson I have ever met. Proving that you can be a successful business hippy.

To Amy Morse, an amazing copywriter, who helped me out of a few copy writing paralysis holes. Sometimes you need someone to fish you out of trouble. You did an admirable job.

There are so many of you to thank for your help on the book. For the case studies, the peer reviewing, the wisdom and the knowledge. To be part of such a wonderful movement of people all trying to make a positive difference to the world of work is truly humbling. And so here's to:

Loughlin Hickey and Soulla Kyriacou,
    Blueprint for Better Business
Ken Shuttleworth and Camilla Neave, MAKE architects
Razeea Lemaignen and Jason Sloan, GSK
Natalie Sigona, BAE Systems
Cary Cooper, Robertson Cooper
Mark Catchlove, Herman Miller
Phil Wilcox, Emotion @ Work
Emma Mamo, Mind
Ben Channon, The Architects' Mental Wellbeing Forum
Henry Stewart, Happy Ltd
Justin Varney, Business in the Community

Richard Roberts, Pure Planet
Kerry Wekelo, Actualize Consulting
Fiona Hunter, Brewdog
Richard Bonner, Arcadis
Charlotte Davies, Investors in People
Louella Ibekwe, The Insolvency Service
Michael Smyth, GRAHAM
Anna Meller, Sustainable Working Ltd
Ruth Gawthorpe, The Smart Working Revolution
Liese Lord, The Lightbulb Tree
Katrina Stamp, Flock Associates Ltd
Dr Kerstin Sailer, brainybirdz
Su Menzies-Runciman, Ventures with Vision
Jo Thresher, Better with Money Ltd
Jane Ginnever, Shift Consultancy Ltd
Jayne Harrison, Peak Potential Consulting Ltd
James Routledge, Sanctus
Clare Pass and Rachael Bushby,
    Dragonfly: Impact Education

To all of the leaders, who I have had the pleasure to work with and work alongside on leadership development programmes. You helped me learn so much about leadership and learning, and about what it takes to make people truly happy.

Thank you to the teams I've led. I didn't always get it right, but I learned so much from you. Through your dedication, commitment to quality and commitment to each other.

And thank you to the team at LID Publishing. Especially to Alex Boudreault-Manos for digging me up to write this book in the first place and to Sara Taheri, Susan Furber and Francesca Stainer for all of the guidance and support you've given me along the way.

A MODERN DAY
LEADERSHIP TALE

Sam has got a busy day. Her diary is manic, as always, and she's got a breakfast meeting at 7.30am. Her husband has got the kids, although he's got a morning meeting too, and he's panicking about being late.

She sends some urgent emails on the train, and gets to her meeting having done no prep. She doesn't feel she can contribute too much in the meeting, which is about a flurry of bad Glassdoor reviews they've recently had. No one really understands how Glassdoor works, and so they agree to meet at a later date when they've got a bit more information. The meeting has been a waste of time.

Sam flies off to her next meeting, reading the agenda on the way. It's her monthly team meeting and everyone seems a bit sombre, so she asks if they are all OK, and they say "yes". That's that, then. The team explains what they've got going on; there's a lot, and Sam is wondering how they'll get it all done. They're too busy and they're working long hours. Sam knows this is not sustainable, but she doesn't know how to change things at the moment. One team member in particular looks a bit down, and Sam makes a mental note to catch up with them later.

Sam has a project meeting, which she finally leaves at 2.30pm, having missed lunch and drunk lots of coffee. The meeting was tough. Everyone seemed pretty defensive, and they didn't conclude much. Another follow-up meeting is needed.

Sam goes to look for the team member who seemed down but gets collared. A colleague needs her help. Then she needs to get to another meeting with a disgruntled client. She's not looking forward to it.

She manages to console the client, but they aren't happy. Her team has dropped a few balls, and she knows why: they're overstretched. Sam's phone rings. It's her boss. He has seemed a bit stressed lately and is worried about money. He wants a full breakdown of all team expenditures including costs, but Sam hasn't had the time to prepare it recently. Sam agrees to do it that night, and as she puts the phone down, she wonders when she's going to fit it in. She was supposed to be at the gym.

Sam arrives late for school pick-up. The kids are pleased to see her, so that's something. They don't want to go to After School Club anymore though. Sam finds out that someone is bullying her daughter and that it's upsetting her. She reassures her and says she'll speak to the teacher tomorrow.

Sam and the kids get home, and they have dinner. She puts them to bed and starts working. Her husband gets home and she vaguely acknowledges him, but it's 8pm and she's got a lot to do. She quickly looks at her emails: there are 126 unread. Sam's heart sinks again. She's had a resignation from the employee she didn't manage to see today. Her best person. She feels guilty. She should have picked that up sooner.

Sam grabs a glass of wine, works her way through the report, and thinks about what she's got on tomorrow. It's going to be another busy day.

Does any of this sound familiar to you? Too much work, unhappy team members, customer complaints, frustrated bosses and unproductive meetings? Although it's not always like this, work can be challenging and can place unrealistic demands on people.

In Sam's story, no one was happy. Not Sam, her team, her boss, her husband, the kids or her peers. Yet we work like this all the time. In the short-term it can feel mildly uncomfortable. In the long-term it can affect our health.

Sam was two months away from breaking. Her doctor wanted to sign her off with stress, but the thought of her boss thinking she had stress was awful. She took two weeks off in the end for the 'flu'. She needed a break. Two weeks wasn't enough, but what else could she do, she had so much on.

No one saw that Sam was struggling. She was a powerhouse. In fact, her team would often compliment her on how well she managed her work and home life – she seemed to have it all figured out. The truth was that although Sam was happy, she didn't recognize the impact that work was having on her. Her boss caused her a constant low level of anxiety, as he always seemed fixated on what wasn't working, and her team had too much on. Trying to figure out how to get rid of work was proving challenging, though. Sam wasn't seeing her family, her relationship was being affected, her kids missed her, and she was doing nothing to look after her health and wellbeing. She used to go to the gym and have regular chiropractic appointments; she would take time out to chill and see her friends. She didn't do much of that anymore. She was either working, looking after the kids or crashing through exhaustion. If she had a gap, she'd be on her phone, looking aimlessly at social media.

Sam needed more support from her boss and her peers, and clearer boundaries around how she was prepared to work. When she had time to reflect, she realized that she needed greater meaning in her life. She was working hard, but it didn't seem as though her contribution was being noticed. What was the point? What was the purpose of her work? If it was simply to make more money for the shareholders, that wasn't enough.

INTRODUCTION

What's the Big Idea?

This book is about wellbeing. And that's because it's the big missing link that's stopping us – as people and as organizations – from fulfilling our potential and from staying well.

When I talk about wellbeing, I refer to it in the most holistic of senses. Beyond purely physical and mental health, and the avoidance of ill health, wellbeing is more sophisticated than that.

It's about achieving balance in all aspects of our lives. Physical health and avoiding illness are obviously important to wellbeing, most of us are aware of that, but that's not enough to keep us flourishing.

Wellbeing is about nourishing a spectrum of human needs: physical, social, psychological, emotional and, for some, spiritual. It's the myriad of needs that, when in balance, lead us to feeling our best.

Yet modern day life, at work and at home, makes it hard for us to stay in balance, to pay attention to our needs, to make sure we're achieving what we want from our lives and to keep every part of us nourished. Not least because we don't understand how to.

Very few of us have ever been educated about how we operate as humans, how to look after ourselves, how to understand our own needs and how to satisfy them. And most of us have little to no understanding of the working of our minds, the centrifugal force behind all of our day-to-day decisions – the decisions we make that contribute to our performance and our wellbeing.

So it stands to reason that if we become more consciously aware of who we are and how to take better care of our needs, we will take better care of our wellbeing.

Why Does It Matter?

Improving and maintaining our wellbeing matters for a number of reasons, not least because when our wellbeing is not where it should be, it affects our performance at work. This can also have detrimental effects on our health, on our ability to achieve what we want to, on our relationships and on our ability to lead. When our wellbeing isn't in balance, it can affect our outlook on life, our motivation levels and our mental clarity. It can create barriers and blockages that get in the way of us being at our best and achieving what we are capable of. It can also lead to physical illness.

At an organizational level, when people don't feel well, this slows down progress, negatively affects productivity and tends to lead to higher levels of absence and attrition.

What Will This Book Cover?

It won't deal with the knowns, like nutrition, exercise and sleep. Most of us know these are good for us, and there is already plenty of information out there on those topics.

The focus of this book is on what is less clear about wellbeing: how we can fulfil our intrinsic needs as humans, such as our need for relationships, our need for meaning and our ability to take better care of our mental health. It's these social, emotional and psychological needs that we've never properly learned how to harness.

In this book, you'll learn about the meaning of wellbeing in a modern day context; why it's a central component to employee and organizational performance; and how to galvanize it in yourself and others.

The most successful teams understand that it's not just all about high performance – you might already be a high performer. Unless you look after your wellbeing too, your performance is unlikely to be sustained. This will impact you, and it will impact the people around you.

Unless you understand how to take better care of yourself and how to create the conditions that enable others to do the same, your long-term health, performance and growth are at risk.

The world of work is changing more rapidly than ever and, as a leader, you need to recognize what that means for the way in which you and others work.

In the chapters that follow, you will learn about how 'the conscious effect' will help you become more aware of yourself and others. This means you can create the conditions both in yourself and in the workplace that lead to high performance – high performance that is achieved in a responsible way. This combination of becoming more self-aware and connected to others will help you achieve more.

And if you are one of the organizations or individuals already making progress in this area, you'll get to learn more about how to build on what you're already doing well.

Who Is the Book For?

You might be an aspiring leader; you might be an already high-performing leader. This book is for people who want to make a change. Who want to be at their best. Who can see the consequences of the chaos around us and who want to stay focused and able to make a positive difference. Who want their leadership skills to match the modern workplace. Who want to be more conscious about how they lead themselves and others, and who want to create a more sustainable environment for others to work in.

Why I Wrote This Book

I spent my career working in human resources (HR), and I loved it. When the recession hit in 2008, things got harder. I went from looking at recruitment and rewards to searching for cost cuts. My job became about letting people go, removing non-essential spending, and tightening up policies. Everyone was under pressure to do more with less.

The leaders had to work harder to generate revenue, and employees had to give more discretionary effort and work longer hours. It was all hands on deck. This was OK in the short term, but the recession was long, and the pressure didn't let up.

I became even more focused on 'creating the best place to work'. I wanted to make sure that despite the circumstances, people were still happy and had the opportunity to progress. Yet it was hard work.

It became the new norm to work long hours. Everyone was working hard. During that time, things became 24/7. Digitalizing transformed the way we worked, and we became even more 'switched on'. Not just because we could answer emails straightaway, but we were being bombarded with constant information and requests. And things were changing constantly.

The relentlessness led to a kind of autopilot. You just had to keep on going. At the same time, we were trying to find ways of making things better. Opportunity opened up all around us. It was exciting and exhausting. Making change happen led to more human problems, trying to influence people who were already saturated.

I didn't realize the extent to which my wellbeing was being affected, even when I Googled 'symptoms of a nervous breakdown' on the train home one evening. A few months later, I reached burnout. It was one of the most devastating experiences of my life. I had always considered myself to be resilient, robust, driven and happy.

All of a sudden, I lost my confidence and couldn't think straight. I'd flatlined.

It was at that point that I recognized I needed to change. I'd worked in leadership development for years, but no amount of developing leaders gave me the knowledge I needed to keep my own wellbeing in balance – and that of those around me. I was so focused on performance that my wellbeing suffered. I knew a lot about communication, team performance, high performance, change, interpersonal skills, leadership styles and how to manage difficult conversations. The missing link was wellbeing. I was missing the self-care and self-knowledge that I needed to keep myself on track and growing personally.

This is when I realized there was another way: a more conscious and responsible way of leading high performance. I developed the Conscious Leadership model and felt that I needed to write this book to make sure future and current leaders didn't end up in the same place I had. For their own sake and that of their teams.

Since my own experience, I have spoken to countless people who have had similar experiences or who are struggling. It's not just the overwhelm and conflict we face in work, it's the problems we're facing around us. Politics, climate change, the state of the economy – it all creates uncertainty and for many, anxiety. And we want to do more to fix it. Either for our own benefit or for the benefit of society. We're becoming more purpose driven. In work and outside of it.

Since starting up my own company, I've been encouraged to find that there are many organizations and individuals who are doing great things. Who recognize the importance of conscious leadership, of taking a more responsible approach, and who want to make a bigger and more positive difference. Not just for their own wellbeing, but for the wellbeing of others too.

The truth is, we can achieve high performance in our organizations, but it will only be sustainable if we figure out how to take care of wellbeing too.

Times Are Changing

Although the recession presented us with challenges that many of us hadn't faced in our careers, the world is continuing to change at a rapid pace, and we've got a lot to learn about how to thrive in this new era.

The economy is in a constant state of flux, and it's fair to say that the political and economic landscape is volatile. It's affecting investment, logistics, talent supply, the environment, security, governance – everything seems to be constantly on the move. Some of these changes are great for business and great for society, and some make it harder to operate. Regardless, organizations are constantly having to change in response. It means a new, more agile and adaptive skill set is required to function in the modern world of work.

And the shift in technology is phenomenal too. We are facing the 'Fourth Industrial Revolution'. It's predicted that almost half of current jobs are subject to potential automation[1] and although robots aren't quite set to take over the world, we're definitely going to be sharing our planet with a lot of bionic friends in the not-so-distant future. Those who watched in awe as Keanu Reeves navigated *The Matrix* all those years ago only have to turn on their phones now to immerse themselves in a digital world where social media is the new Big Brother.[2]

We're going to need to develop a new skill set to function in the new world, as humans and technology come closer together.

Employee expectations are changing too.[3] They want employers who are responsible, who have integrity, who treat them as adults, and who can support their growth and development. And they want greater flexibility. People are shifting to portfolio careers and self-employment[4], and the gig economy is supposedly upon us.[5] Technology now means we don't even need a desk or an office – people can work from anywhere at any time. And many of them will want to.

And I'm not just talking about millennials. I believe that most people want or would benefit from what the millennials are asking for, if they are just brave enough to ask for it.

As talent shifts its expectations, employers will need to shift theirs. This presents fantastic opportunities to shape new working environments. Making these changes doesn't lessen the expectations that we have for people to perform – in fact, it should actually boost them.

Organizations who care more will win the best talent, and they'll achieve the greatest success.

And there's no excuse for not knowing what to do to make things better. We now have a far greater understanding of people, of neuroscience, and of what leads to the best performance and wellbeing, and we have the technology to better support ourselves.

We can now be more responsible, and any organization or leader who doesn't see the role they can play in this evolution is missing something. We all have a duty to leave this planet, and the people on it, in a better state than in which we found them. We have a duty to our children, and a duty to each other.

It's called consciousness: the whole purpose of this book. Through waking up, working better together, learning the new skills that are required to function in our evolving world and through recognizing that we can all make a positive difference, we will run better organizations and lead better lives.

Wellbeing as the Foundation for Performance

Driving performance and productivity has been at the fore-front of organizations for a long time. Yet we've worked so hard for so long now that we've seen the consequences, with productivity being negatively affected and people getting sick – both mentally and physically.

We're starting to recognize that simply putting in more effort doesn't lead to greater performance. In fact, there's now growing evidence to show that working long hours actually has a detrimental effect on our performance.[6]

So how do you create greater levels of performance, keep productivity high, and get more out of people, without getting them to do more? The answer is that you have to change.

How about a world where we put more into our employees than we take out? To enable them to fulfill more of their potential.

We haven't learned how to take care of ourselves and our people well enough. When people take care of themselves, and take care of each other, they are happier, more satis-fied and more creative. When people feel well, they produce better results.[7] We're not bad people, we've just focused on the wrong things for too long. We've put people on the Moon, created autonomous cars and built buildings that hit the clouds, yet we haven't figured out how to take care of ourselves and how to optimize the way we work. There is a certain irony to that.

I spoke to Perry Timms, an HR Futurist, about this, and he rightly said, "We're living a smartphone existence, where our energy is depleted by the end of the day and where our workplaces are making us sick. We need to redesign the world of work."

And there are good commercial reasons for us to get to grips with this whole wellbeing thing. Cary Cooper (a bit of a superstar in this field) told me that from his extensive experience, the biggest priorities for employers right now are retaining their people and managing sickness. It's a real problem for them and it's slowing organizations down. Cary explained that although there is a lot of great work being done around mental health, we shouldn't just be focusing on educating people about mental illness. Wellbeing can prevent mental health issues, but there is a lot more to wellbeing than that.

And as long as taking care of wellbeing is a bolt-on activity, something that HR does, or a token activity to raise awareness of the odd national awareness-building day, it won't make a difference. Supporting wellbeing should flow through the fibres of an organization and sit as a core objective or foundational activity that drives the culture and the performance of that organization.

The Paradox of Working Life

Sitting in my kitchen one day, I noticed the irony that was sitting on my windowsill. We have an array of supplements: pre- and probiotics, multivitamins, D3, milk thistle, oil of evening primrose, and we take them as often as we remember in a bid to stay healthy. Yet right next to all that nourishment were the kid's advent calendars, or 24 days of sugar – and advent calendars are definitely bigger than they used to be. And then it dawned on me. The sweets next to the vitamins reflected the paradox of our working lives.

Employers do a lot that is good. They offer people money in exchange for effort (sometimes really good money), they provide a host of different benefits, an office (sometimes quite nice offices) and various tools that people need to do their job, they invest money in training and development, and they provide other rewards for hard work.

So, they pour all of these lovely vitamins in (some better quality than others), and then they add the sugar. The long working hours, the untrained managers, the lack of clear direction, the lack of opportunity for progression, and the unrealistic expectations.

They put some good things in, but then they pour in the bad stuff. Yet they expect their employees to be fit, healthy and well all of the time, and to function at their best round the clock.

You know that if you have too much sugar it's not good for your health. Yet how many leaders know what 'workplace sugar' they're feeding people?

It's a paradox. Yet unless everyone wakes up and becomes more consciously aware of the impact this sugar is having on them, their health and ultimately their performance, we're heading for some serious long-term health problems.

Are you feeding people too much sugar?

Getting to Know Wellbeing

The wellbeing industry is flooded with companies trying to help employers 'care' more, and you can see why. In the UK alone, the statistics are worrying:

- Mental health is costing:
  > employers between £33 billion and £42 billion per year (based on sickness absence, staff turnover and presenteeism)[8]
  > the economy between £74 billion and £99 billion per year[9]
- 24% of employees think their job negatively affects their mental health[10]
- 1 in 5 employees report feeling exhausted at work[11]
- The UK has the lowest productivity of all the G7 countries[12]
- Only 18% of people are supposedly engaged at work[13]

Something is going very wrong. Employers are feeling the strain of poor wellbeing every day – and they don't seem to be able to fix it.

For a long time now, employers have been focused on helping people back to work when they get sick, but as we've said before, wellbeing is more than just the avoidance of ill health. In a research report I read,[14] wellbeing was described as "the balance point between an individual's resource pool and the challenges faced." But how conscious are we at any one time of where our resource pool is at? I'm fascinated by Carol Ryff's work, as she has spent her life studying the factors that significantly contribute to the quality of our lives and wellbeing. She defined psychological wellbeing in particular as having six key dimensions: self-acceptance; control over our surroundings; positive relationships with others; autonomy; personal growth; and life purpose.[15]

And when we look at wellbeing from a holistic perspective, it's absolutely about these things. When you consider what's going on in your life when you're feeling at your best, you'd probably agree that some of these aspects are in balance.

Yet there are still many organizations trying to improve wellbeing through providing occupational health and employee assistance programmes, and by promoting 'awareness days'. I'm not saying these are wrong – they help. They are just part of the fix, though. Unless we create good conditions for people to work in, activities like these won't make a difference. No amount of gym memberships, dental health policies and financial education will fix poor management, outdated working practices and long hours. They are simply sticking plasters on a more fundamental problem.

Wellbeing should be seen as a continuum, with illness at one end and wellness sitting at the other. If we only ever take a curative approach to fixing wellbeing, offering support when someone has reached the point where they are unwell or too stressed, we're losing the opportunity to boost and maintain performance when people feel good.

When we're feeling well, we tend to be more motivated, engaged and more positively focused. When we are unwell (either mentally or physically), the opposite is true. We'll tend to be more negative, have lower energy, and be less productive and engaged.

The Chartered Institute of Personnel and Development (CIPD) 2018 Health and Wellbeing at Work Report showed that two-fifths of organizations have a standalone wellbeing strategy.[16] This is great news, but it's not just about having the strategy. It's about making sure the strategy is built on the right foundations.

Although there is an abundance of yoga classes, nutrition workshops and mindfulness sessions being organized, in a 'stressed' environment these will create momentary fixes. Unless organizations critically assess how healthy the culture is to start with, and how enabled people are to take better care of themselves and the way they work, they are likely to miss the point. And taking care of yourself isn't just about physical acts; it's about the way we think that matters too. Which means that building self-knowledge is equally as important.

Planning Your Approach to Wellbeing

In an ideal world, all organizations would understand the importance of investing in wellbeing, as they would recognize it as the right thing to do from a moral perspective. They wouldn't need a business case to justify investment.

Yet in a commercial world, and while we're trying to figure out what works, tracking progress is a good way of being sure that our efforts are worth it.

To date, some studies have shown that investing in wellbeing hasn't proven successful.[17] There is other evidence to show how it has positively impacted the bottom line. In order to make sure that your wellbeing efforts make a positive difference, there are certain things to consider:

1. Know what your starting point is – unless you know what you are trying to improve and how you are going to monitor progress, demonstrating ROI will be difficult.
2. Know where you are trying to get to – create a vision for the future, the 'why' behind what you're doing and what you want to achieve from any investment. It will be the guiding light for your efforts.

3. Look at all aspects of wellbeing – this means setting a strategy which, over time, will consider the holistic elements of wellbeing: physical, psychological and social.
4. Get leadership buy-in – no amount of effort on the part of HR or the wellbeing team is going to make a difference if the leadership team has not bought in. They need to be involved from the earliest stages.
5. Involve employees – ask them what would make a positive difference to their working life. Don't limit it to benefits. Ask them about how they want to work, and what else would help them to do their best.

There are a number of companies that on the face of it seem to be getting it right.

Accenture's investment in wellbeing led to a number of improvements, including: an 8%[18] increase in employee engagement; 9,000 hours' reduction of absenteeism; and an increase in productivity of 3%. Based on research carried out by the Human Capital Management Institute, companies that invest just US$1 per person on wellbeing can outperform their peers and experience a 11.7% productivity gain.[19]

And a large Australian fire and rescue service ran mental health training with their managers and achieved an ROI of £9.98 for each pound spent. This was said to be largely due to a reduction in sickness absence.[20]

Whatever the aim of your wellbeing efforts, knowing your starting point is crucial and having a clear 'why' will create a more compelling purpose for others to get behind. Wellbeing shouldn't be something owned by a central business function; it should be owned by every single person in the organization, even if you as leaders sometimes need to take the first step.

Wellbeing Starts with the Leader

Wellbeing starts with the leaders, because unless healthy behaviours are being role-modelled by those who are responsible for leading everyone else, we start on shaky foundations.

This is where Conscious Leadership comes in, and that's the real focus of this book. When leaders become more consciously aware of their own and others' needs, and of how to take better care of them, they create working environments that people want to be a part of – and then I'd argue you don't even need a wellbeing strategy. The relationships between leaders and their people have such a significant impact on individual wellbeing, that they are central to building an effective approach to wellbeing.

Additionally, leaders who are conscious know that in order to get the best from anyone, including themselves, working on balance and personal development has a big impact on the way we feel, and therefore on our performance.

Conscious Leadership is about being self aware and deepening our self-knowledge. It's also about building a culture of togetherness, purpose, resilience and personal growth. It means learning to better manage our own internal conditions as well as creating the nourishing conditions in which others can grow and thrive too. This balance of internal and external work is crucial. You can work on yourself, but if you're working in a toxic or demanding environment, there's only so much progress that will be possible. And the external environment might be great, but if you're riddled with limiting beliefs and lacking in confidence or if you're working too hard, you are unlikely to thrive. Both aspects – what goes on in our heads and what goes on around us – impact how well we are, and therefore how well we perform.

Being More Conscious

When you become more conscious, you are more self-aware, and have greater self-knowledge. Through paying greater attention to who you are and how you are thinking, feeling and acting, and whether it's getting you what you want and need, you can get clearer about what to do. It leads to better decisions and enables you to make changes – to positively improve your life. Unless you're conscious, change is unlikely. When we make changes as a consequence of self-awareness, we can take better care of our wellbeing and performance. We can grow.

Through recognizing your needs, your patterns of working, of being, and how you impact others, you can make better decisions and achieve better results. In your work and your relationships.

Others matter too. You can only effectively lead others to deliver successful outcomes if you understand people and what they need. It means paying attention to them, listening, noticing and acting on what you see and hear around you. All essential traits of a good leader.

This is what I refer to as Conscious Intelligence. It's a skill that you can grow through greater conscious awareness of yourself and of people – of humans – and how they work. When we work on Conscious Intelligence, we work on wellbeing too.

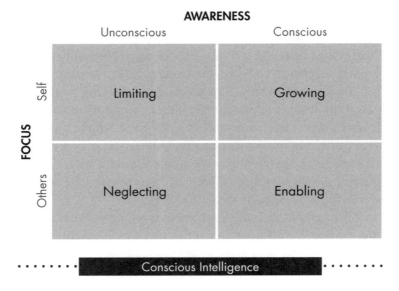

Explaining Conscious Leadership

When we become more conscious of ourselves and of others, we are better placed to be good leaders. It's this understanding that enables us to more fully appreciate what leads to human flourishing. It's all too easy to stay on automatic pilot at work, keeping our fingers crossed that everyone is OK, and making changes and requests that we presume that everyone will be happy with.

Yet, being human is complex. It's the one problem in life we haven't solved. And being human can make us very miserable if we don't learn how to do it effectively. We put immense pressure on ourselves to be 'awesome humans' – and it can take its toll. Many of the ancient philosophers would probably frown upon us. Maybe a bit of stoicism would help us. According to Seneca, "What need is there to weep over parts of life? The whole of life calls for tears."

Well, maybe that's taking things a bit too far, and we need to be able to get out of bed in the morning, so what's the alternative to anticipating the worst possible outcomes? It means figuring out 'what it is to be human' and taking action to change the aspects of ourselves that are not helping us or others.

We're not taught about it at school, we get very little training on it at work, and then we're expected to turn up as a leader and act as a pseudo-psychologist, understanding the interplay between human beings and what brings out the best in them. We are expected to know how to motivate other people, when half the time we can't even motivate ourselves to do the things we need to.

And we need to make sure we keep people interested, engaged, developing and 'in the office', while at the same time supporting everyone through the working challenges they face and sometimes the life challenges that are getting in the way of them being 'present'.

We're expected to know how to get the best out of others when we don't even know if we're getting the best out of ourselves. Very few of us really understand ourselves.

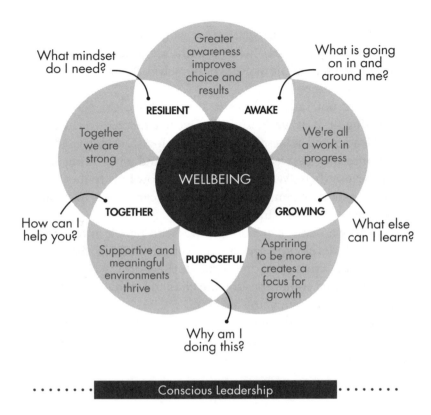

This is where Conscious Leadership can help us. A set of five crucial foundations that allow us to create the internal (within us) and external (around us) conditions to thrive. These internal and external conditions lead to better individual and organizational wellbeing. The five areas overlap, with the central overlap being where we achieve wellbeing. I developed this model based on my experience of seeing what makes people happy and well at work, and much of the research I've done since has reinforced my view.

Crucial to Conscious Leadership is being **awake**. Leaders need to recognize that the behaviour they model drives the culture that they operate in, and therefore the way that employees behave and feel. Only through an ongoing commitment to developing greater self-awareness, to being able to critically assess and manage ourselves, and through learning from our experiences can we hope to understand our impact as leaders. As well as being a better role model, you are likely to learn what leads to your own wellbeing. A happier and healthier you will lead to a happier and healthier team.

Once we become more awake, we can start to build our resilience. The world around us will continue to change and we will continue to be bombarded with everything the world has to throw at us. To survive, and ideally to thrive, we must be **resilient**. This is largely about the mindset we show up to the world with. It's the difference between us floundering and flourishing. It enables us to bounce back in times of adversity and provides the leadership and mental toughness we need to keep going, even in times of difficultly. Resilience is an essential trait for leaders, as is their ability to develop resilience in the people they lead.

Leaders have started to figure out that working with their people, not commanding them, will achieve the best results. Treating people as adults and empowering them is the key to high performance, but also to helping others to feel valued and as though they can bring their best self to work. Leaders who create environments where people feel safe to express themselves and who support each other, to build healthy and thriving cultures. Removing fear, getting out of people's way, while keeping people engaged in what is going on is at the centre of working **together**.

People want to find meaning in their work and for there to be **purpose** behind what they are doing. When you raise the consciousness of the organization, you get everyone focused around a central and compelling purpose. This gives direction and builds commitment. When organizations have a clear and emotionally compelling 'why' to drive their efforts, people know what they need to do to make a positive difference. When we know we're making a valued contribution, it inspires us to do more.

Yet without constant learning and the belief that effort and focus will lead to better results, it supresses progress. Leaders who nurture a **growth** mindset, one which isn't afraid of challenge, of doing things you haven't done before, of failing and rebuilding, create the space for people to do their best work. They also encourage personal growth, which is borne out of self-awareness.

To be a conscious leader, you need to be awake. You need to be aware of your needs and the needs of others. That way, you can run more responsible and conscious organizations. And you need to intentionally create conscious environments where everyone is responsible for their own wellbeing and the wellbeing of others – building resilience together. Only through doing it together, with clear purpose, and through growth, will you hope to make the most significant and lasting difference.

You're on a Journey

What you notice when you start to learn more about yourself is that this is a journey. The more you learn, the more you question, and so the journey continues.

This book will encourage you towards a mindset that will make you feel better This isn't about wholescale change and overnight transformation. It's about becoming more consciously aware of who you are, how you behave, and the impact that has on yourself and others. It's about learning about how your mind works, what motivates people, what suppresses people's performance, what brings out our best, our instinctual needs, and what it means to be human.

This is about getting the programming that drives the human machine working better, because when you recognize that it's people who make organizations work – starting with the individual self – you recognize that wellbeing starts there. It starts with the way that you feel every day.

Creating organizational wellbeing isn't about a series of initiatives that seek to educate others on the virtues of how to stay healthy. It's about how leaders show up; it's about how the way they think, feel, act and encourage others to act creates a culture in which people feel well.

I have written this book as a series of lessons that will help you to make incremental changes. Each lesson will help you to make improvements – to yourself as a leader and to the environment that your people work in. Don't expect the changes to happen overnight. This is deep work. Becoming more conscious is just the starting point. Then starts the journey of growth and change.

In each section of the book you'll find 'the big conscious question'. This is the question you should be asking yourself. Asking yourself as a leader and as a person. And you should be encouraging your team to ask it of themselves too.

There is a movement of people trying to help solve this challenge, and I'll introduce you to some of them throughout this book. We are all in this together, and we need to make a united effort to become more conscious. For a better us and a better world. Welcome to the movement.

TOGETHER

You Need to
Feel Connected

The Big Conscious Question: How Can I Help You?

Humans crave social connection and a sense of belonging. The relationships you have, and how psychologically safe you feel, all have an impact on your wellbeing and how you perform at work. This is why leaders who create a sense of togetherness, stand a good chance of achieving good results.

Yet a lot of what you experience at work can fail to satisfy these needs. People can feel threatened when leaders are unable to or don't pay enough attention to creating that sense of community or support for one another. People can become frustrated, apathetic, and disengaged, and suffer from poor mental wellbeing if they do not feel trusted and empowered, or if there are barriers to being able to collaborate effectively with others. This in turn affects performance.

Leaders who are more conscious of these human needs pay attention to relationships and to creating a harmonious environment in which people can support each other. When you don't have to fear failing or making mistakes, when everyone is treated as equal, and when people are aware of and are encouraged to support each other's needs, it creates healthy, enabling work environments in which people are encouraged to be themselves and work for the greater good.

This means challenging the traditional hierarchies seen in the workplace. It means leaders understanding that their role is to enable and support their people, rather than operating as 'parents' who tell others what do to and who punitively point out where people are not performing as they'd like them to. The idea that employees will fit a 'standard' mould, will do as they are told, and should not question the status quo is an outdated concept. Although many leaders know this, there are still many operating practices and leaders that default to this approach.

As with any community, trust needs to form one of the basic operating principles. Leaders must recruit people they are willing to trust and empower, give them flexibility to work in a way that suits their needs, and give them the freedom to co-create solutions. When leaders do this, it leads to more honest dialogue, improved engagement and employees taking greater ownership for results. It also creates an environment where team members are more likely to trust each other. Everyone is in it together.

In part, it is down to an emotional connection and understanding of others, which leads to better-quality relationships. Leaders who encourage collaboration are more likely to achieve high performance. Given that we depend on relationships to achieve much of our day-to-day work, galvanizing relationships and nurturing an environment that strengthens the connection between people enhances performance, but it also improves our wellbeing. It's common sense. When our relationships are good, we feel better.

And when you feel valued and included, it nourishes your wellbeing too. It's this emotional connection to your environment that has a positive impact on the way you feel, your mental health and your motivation to do your best work.

As many of you spend the majority of your time at work, being emotionally connected to what you are doing and who you work with is important. It can have a significant impact on your energy levels, both inside and outside of work.

I have the pleasure of working with Gary Gill through Engage for Success, an organization that helps employers build employee engagement in the workplace. Gary believes that engaged employees are those who tend to be emotionally attached to their jobs, to the work that they do and to the organization itself. The relationships they hold and the part they play in the community are significant contributors to their level of engagement – to that emotional attachment.

We all find emotional attachment in our own ways based on our own individual values, backgrounds and experience. When leaders recognize this and foster a community of diverse individuals, they unleash the magic of individuality in the organization. It means letting people bring their authentic selves to work and encouraging the diversity of ideas that stems from different experiences and views of life. When people can be themselves at work, when they can express their thoughts and ideas, they are more likely to be emotionally connected to the team and their work. When leaders become more consciously aware of this, they can be more intentional about building a community of people who want to work together, grow together, and who build on each others ideas.

LESSON 1

Work in Partnership with People

Although 'command-and-control' leadership may conjure up visions of political dictators and narcissistic control freaks, there is a far less extreme and far more common form of command-and-control leadership affecting performance and wellbeing in the workplace today.

When leaders simply 'command' others rather than creating opportunities for two-way dialogue, and when there is one prescribed way of doing things, it leads to learned helplessness among employees, and they become unable to think for themselves.

Many leaders adopt this 'tell' approach to leadership without realizing it, often because of time pressure or the belief that they are 'in charge'. This makes them less likely to build relationships with their people. Yet today's employees want to have control over their work and their results and they want a voice. Leaders need to stay close enough to provide support but far enough away to give others the space to think, grow and take responsibility for their own results. This is what's behind the idea of 'partnership'. It's leaders and employees working together, to get things done and to co-create ideas for improvement. Research shows us that when followers feel they are part of the same group as the leader, they are more likely to be receptive to the leader's propositions and ideas.[21] Yet, often leaders form one group in an organization and employees form another.

Historically, leadership was more about giving orders. This was the best way to drive efficiency, run standardized processes and limit the risk of people getting things wrong. There wasn't as much requirement for people to think for themselves, and the 'man' at the top would know what was needed to keep things running effectively. That's why they were leaders.

Much has changed over the years and nowadays, in a working environment that is constantly evolving and where the opportunity for improvement and innovation is expanding, we're expecting more from employees. They need to be agile, innovative and resilient and they need to be committed, hard-working and focused. And employees have expectations too. Generally speaking, they want to have more say, have influence over the shape of their role, find meaning in their work, and be involved in the decisions that impact them every day.

They want to be treated like adults. The role of modern leaders therefore becomes more about keeping the team energized and focused, coordinating and organizing group efforts, and acting more as a coach than a 'commander'. It requires the leader to understand the team members' various strengths and interests, and to engage them in what is going to motivate them. It requires a more open dialogue. Through working in partnership as a leader, you remove any unnecessary hierarchy and empower others to take ownership for making decisions too. This freedom can make a significant and positive difference to the mental health and performance of the team and the leader.

How to Create an Environment of Partnership

1. Stay involved – avoid working outside of the team and solving problems alone. Get the team involved and be the first to work collaboratively with others in the team.
2. Talk about partnership – have an open discussion about what partnership means. Ask the team about how they want to contribute, how ideas should be developed and how everyone can better support each other.

3. Watch your behaviour – start noticing how often you tell the team what to do or give them a direct instruction. Notice if you provide an opportunity for discussion and whether you take on board other people's views.

Leadership Myths
1. Leaders are there to tell others what to do.
2. Leaders and employees need to keep their distance.

Get Conscious
Is it your role to be in command of your team? How closely do you work with individuals on the team? How comfortable do you feel about being a partner to your team? How could this partnership shift the dynamics of how the team works. How would it shift your behaviour? What needs to change for you to feel you can partner with team members?

LESSON 2

Leaders Are Enablers

Some leaders already work in partnership with their people, yet many of us have different views of what it means to be a leader. That's why it's important to define what successful leadership looks like in the modern age. When we look at the words associated with the term 'leadership', it's interesting to see that many outdated leadership characteristics are still seen as being relevant, such as 'administration' and 'power'.[22,23]

In an increasingly complex and pressured world, leaders can't do everything and be everywhere, and this means depending on the team, effectively utilizing the talents of its members. This doesn't mean allowing people to do whatever they want, whenever they want. It means recognizing that others have good thoughts and ideas, and that enabling those ideas makes sense.

It can be difficult, especially as a new leader, to understand how to enable others to work effectively.

Leaders who enable understand that they are there to leverage the talents of others, which means understanding what those talents are and making sure people are being developed to get even better. They know that others can make good decisions as long as they understand the parameters in which to make those decisions, and that they will not always be best placed to help a team member solve a problem. This is why they encourage the members to gather knowledge from outside the team, connecting them with other resources and people who may be of value.

Enabling leaders feel comfortable with others taking risks. When an employee wants to try out a new idea or to focus some of their time on personal development rather than pure delivery, an enabling leader will give them the chance to do that, offering initial guidance, and supporting them along the way.

They create an environment that removes as many barriers to people doing their jobs effectively as possible. That's because they understand that the working environment can place unnecessary stressors in the way, and they work hard to get these shifted. Whether that be process or people issues, they are always scanning the horizon for what may be affecting their people, their performance and their wellbeing (or stress levels as some leaders see it). Whether it's about having the right resource, changing systems or dealing with internal wranglings, they craft an environment that clears a path for the team to make progress.

The same as a sports coach down on the sports field, enabling leaders recognize the factors that either impede or accelerate the team. Once upon a time, that was purely about efficiency in most organizations; now it's about people's individual wellbeing too.

How Can You Become a More Enabling Leader?

1. Keep your eyes open – although you'll probably have plenty of your own work to do, keep an eye on what's getting in the way of the team being able to do their best work. And have the courage to remove the blockers (see Lesson 50: Leaders Need Courage).
2. Connect people up – there are often situations where people outside of the team or the organization can bring huge value to the knowledge and development of the team. Look out for opportunities to connect the team to others, encouraging them to seek new knowledge to share with the team.

3. Ask what you can do – to help the team. Rather than seeing the team as a resource for you, see everyone as being part of a whole, and consider how you can help others as much as how they can help you.

Leadership Myths

1. Leaders should have all of the knowledge needed to help the team.
2. The team is there as a resource to help the leader to deliver.

Get Conscious

What do you do to enable everyone in the team to perform? In what way do you feel the environment holds the team back – and what can you do about it? Who else could help your team grow and perform? Are there performance problems in the team? If so, to what extent may they be environmental?

LESSON 3

You Need to Feel Safe

'Psychological safety' is a phrase that is bandied about a lot these days, but what does it actually mean? A two-year study carried out by Google identified 'trust' as the most important factor in developing high-performing teams. Paul Santagata, Head of Industry at Google, said: "There's no team without trust." Based on their study, trust is the one thing that high-performing teams have in common: more specifically, the belief that they won't be punished if they make a mistake.[24]

Amy Edmondson, the Novartis Professor of Leadership and Management at the Harvard Business School, a leading authority on psychological safety describes it as having "a shared belief that the team is safe for interpersonal risk taking". When Edmondson was at university studying high-performing teams, she found that better-performing teams seemed to make more mistakes than worse-performing ones. What was interesting was that it wasn't because they actually made more errors, but because they were just better at owning up to them. There was a 'climate of openness' that led to a higher level of performance.[25]

In numerous studies, psychological safety has consistently been shown to play a role in enabling performance because when people feel 'safe', they offer more ideas, admit mistakes, ask for help, and provide feedback. People tend to be more focused on collective goals and problem prevention rather than self-protection. It means being more willing to express yourself instead of disengaging, withdrawing and defending. When people are given the benefit doubt and they don't see a 'down side' to putting across an idea or opinion, it means they are less anxious. It also helps to build confidence as when we know others want to support us and are keen to hear from us, we're more likely to push ourselves to contribute and take on responsibility.

The reason that psychologically safe working environments contribute to wellbeing, is that when people feel free to express themselves without fear of punishment, they experience less anxiety. It means creating a culture where the perceived risk of speaking up is low.[26]

Often, people have a natural tendency to not challenge their superiors (even though those superiors may be unaware of it). Unless leaders are intentional about creating an environment, which encourages everyone to challenge the status quo, identify problems and to suggest ideas that contribute to the well-being of the organization,[27] there are likely to be many opportunities missed.

In environments where there is low tolerance for mistakes and where people are fearful, it leads to unnecessary underlying and ongoing anxiety, which can impact people's health. It can also lead to resignations, poor levels of collaboration,[28] and disengagement, as people feel they don't have enough control over the environment. This can lead to depressed performance.[29]

Take for instance the leader who is criticized when they don't hit sales targets. They put more pressure on the team when make people make mistakes and they criticize them rather than helping them – because they are living in fear themselves. This leads to a vicious cycle of blame and anxiety which drives disengagement, a breakdown in trust, and a negative impact on the well-being of the team.[30]

Leaders who trust, and who recognize that we're all human, create an environment in which the group feel more comfortable and confident to explore and experiment, and to speak openly. For leaders to have that level of confidence in others, it often means building their own confidence first. Unless you as a leader are willing to be challenged and questioned, you are less likely to create a culture of psychological safety.

How to Create Psychological Safety

1. Remove blame – because fear is created by leaders who feel the need to blame others when things don't go according to plan. When you trust employees to do their best and support them when they are off course, they are more likely to succeed.
2. See mistakes as learning – leaders who encourage experimentation and use what doesn't go well as an opportunity to learn and correct course, create a 'safer' space in which people can try out new ideas without fear.
3. Own up to mistakes – being honest about your own flaws as a leader shows a humility that people admire and respect. When leaders can own up to being imperfect, it relieves pressure on others to be perfect too.

Leadership Myths

1. Less mistakes lead to better performance.
2. People need to be blamed to know where to improve.

Get Conscious

How 'safe' do you feel at work? Are you able to admit to mistakes? Would your team own up when something has gone wrong? How would you react? Do you default to blaming? Do you trust your team? Do they trust you? Are people able to speak up without fear of criticism?

LESSON 4

Leaders Are Adults, Not Parents

As a leader, you may find it difficult to decide on your role when it comes to 'looking after' the people you lead. We have grown up in a world where the most senior or experienced figures in our lives were our parents or caregivers, and their role was to look after us. That included telling us what to do, correcting our mistakes and giving us cuddles when we got hurt. Teachers would have played a similar role. They were the governors of our performance and our learning, and the leaders of our earlier lives.

It is unsurprising to discover that the dynamics we experience in our earlier years often unconsciously influence our interactions and relationships when we're older.

Someone whose work was seminal in this area was psychiatrist Eric Berne, who came up with the theory of Transactional Analysis (TA) as a way to explain how we interact with others, and the link to childhood.[31] Bern talked about three ego states that drive our behaviour:

Parent – the attitudes, feelings and behaviours incorporated from parents or caregivers. In this state, adults act out what their parents would have said, felt and done. This parental state can be either nurturing or critical.

Adult – the ability to think and act based on current experience. Normally we are more 'rational', calm and considered in this state and don't feel extreme emotions. This is where we are more likely to interact with another in a curious and empathetic way rather than from a position of blame or point scoring.

Child – the state conjured from feelings and experiences as a child. They may be good or not so good.

You may not consider your past influences, or the 'states' that you adopt when dealing with others, and this is because for the most part our reactions and the way we behave are largely subconscious. It is useful to know about these states, though, as it means we can choose to shift our state if we believe that a different one will serve us better.

Both the parent and child ego states are rooted in the past and our old experiences, whereas the adult state is more concerned with what is going on in the moment. It is, therefore, more effective to remain in the adult state, especially as leaders needing to build effective relationships with the people around them. Although you cannot control someone else's ego state, you can recognize where you and the other person are and make a conscious effort to remain firmly rooted in 'adult'. This is not always easy, as we can automatically react to another person's state and be triggered back into old ways of behaving. However, when we become more consciously aware this is happening, we can learn to adapt our responses.

Sometimes it can be an innocuous comment that triggers us emotionally. It won't be the words that the person used, but the body language that accompanied it that led to your reaction – it wasn't what they said, but how they said it. You can quickly fall into a parent or child response and react negatively, or unhelpfully, based on previous experiences.

Interestingly, words reflect a very small proportion of the meaning we take from interactions and, according to Dr Albert Mehrabian, whose work now plays an important role in our understanding of communication, only 7% of our understanding[32] is formed by words. Tone is far more important, at 38%, but the most important of all is facial expression, at 55%.

So, in the future, give some thought to your reactions. Consider why you are reacting in the way that you are, whether you've fallen into 'parent' or 'child', and how you may be perceived when dealing with others – are you perceived as an adult? And remember, it's rarely the words that have the biggest impact on our understanding of what we hear. It's important for you to understand that when it comes to others perceptions of what you are saying to them too.

How to Encourage Adult Conversations

1. Avoid the need to criticize and punish – and when others react badly around us, listen and be empathetic without feeling the need to 'rescue' or criticize the individual.
2. Don't get defensive – when others take the wrong meaning from what you've said, instead reflect on how your body language or tone may have influenced their perception.
3. Be curious – when you see someone behaving in a highly emotional, guilty or anxious way, try to bring them into the adult state through curious and open questions, using a reassuring tone and body language.

Leadership Myths

1. My parents annoy me; I'm not like them.
2. Words are the most important aspect of communication.

Get Conscious

Do you blame others when things don't work? Do you remain calm and curious when you're not convinced of something? How did your parents or caregivers behave? Were they kind and encouraging or critical? Are there any similarities in how you lead or react to others now?

LESSON 5

Great Leaders Embrace Failure

You've spent days putting together a report for the Board. You attach the document, press 'send' on the email to the Finance Director (FD) and breathe a sigh of relief that it's finally done. It's taken longer than you'd hoped, but you're happy with it.

The following week the FD calls you and questions some of the figures, as the Board doesn't understand them, and they're worried about the dip in performance in the department. It's led to a lengthy debate between the senior leaders, and they want you to provide a report on what's happened. They're already talking about the impact on bonuses.

The team is working really hard and they've performed really well over the course of the year. Things are a bit difficult in the market at the moment and you thought the Board knew that. You're doing everything you can to generate income and you've got some warm leads, but the team is working so hard and you can't expect any more from them. You feel knocked. You're working really hard, everyone is. You wish the Board could be more understanding. Maybe someone could actually help you figure things out rather than persecuting you? They are so unforgiving - maybe you should leave?

Unfortunately, you see things like this happening all of the time. People are doing their best, working hard, yet they are criticized for their efforts. They may not be focusing their efforts in the best way, but rather than being offered words of support and guidance, they are hauled over the coals.

In a more supportive environment, the Board may have queried the figures and called to ask about the drop.

They would have worked with the leader to figure it out and not fallen into crisis. They would have maybe had more trust. In an environment more driven by insecurity and fear, people often forget to give others the benefit of the doubt, acting suspiciously of people and their actions.

These cultures of blame lead people to live in fear and create unnecessary anxiety, which affects individuals' wellbeing.

Not allowing people to make mistakes, fail or have dips in performance can lead to significant levels of anxiety. It can also mean that mistakes get hidden, that people don't speak up when there's a problem, and that they are less likely to experiment and try new things out. This not only affects performance and productivity, but creativity and innovation too. All of those effects are bad for business.

Mistakes and failures and performance dips are an inevitable part of life, and encouraging blameless and constructive feedback reframes failure as an opportunity for learning and development, rather than a setback.[33]

There are numerous success stories that demonstrate this. For example, the failures of Tesla and SpaceX founder Elon Musk have been called "legendary". In 2008, his two companies were on the brink of bankruptcy, and Musk ended up declaring himself bankrupt. As we all know, Tesla went on to achieve great success: in 2018, Tesla had more than 500,000 reservations against its affordable Model3, and SpaceX was paving the way in space exploration.[34]

Steve Jobs, of Apple fame, launched numerous products that failed miserably - the Apple Lisa, Macintosh TV, the Apple III and the Power Mac G4 Cube. In 2018, Apple was the largest tech company in the world, and ranked number one in Fortune 500's most valuable companies.[35] No one sets out to fail. The key is to recognize that 'failure', or performance that doesn't meet expectations, is a crucial part of learning and growth, and when we focus on blame, we take away the opportunity for productive two-way dialogue, which could lead to better performance and growth.

How to Embrace Failure as a Leader

1. Speak openly about the mistakes you've made in your own career – make an event of it. Get the senior leaders together to share 'their biggest ever failure' to break the stigma and show the power of learning from mistakes.
2. Stay calm when people are off track – reassure them that it's normal and review ways in which things can be improved.
3. Trust people to figure things out – encourage the team to be honest about what is not working, so that together you can make adjustments that will improve performance.

Leadership Myths

1. People should achieve high performance constantly.
2. People should get things right first time to achieve the best results.

Get Conscious

Do you overreact to dips in performance? Do you chastise yourself if you don't achieve high performance all of the time? Do you believe that iteration is important in developing new ideas and products? Do you make others feel bad when they make a mistake? Do you encourage two-way discussion when things aren't going well? Are you supportive even when things aren't going well? Do you give up on someone easily if their performance starts to dip?

LESSON 6

The Importance of Autonomy

We've talked about leaders needing to be adults and not parents, yet some leaders take on this parental role, telling others what to do and correcting them for their mistakes. They can also over-manage others.

Micromanagement can take many forms:

- Limiting the amount of challenging work given to employees for fear of it being done incorrectly or not well enough
- Expecting the team to report back on everything they are doing
- Limiting decision-making power among others
- Criticizing the approach and/or decisions of others if it is not what you would have done
- Taking work back if it's not being done as you would want

Although in taking this approach you may manage the risk of errors and stay in control of workflow, it creates other problems that eventually lead to suppressed performance.

Through only giving people the work that you think they can do right now, you remove any challenge or stretch that will allow them to practise new skills or use underdeveloped ones. You will also miss the opportunity to play to possible strengths. This lack of empowerment often leads to a lack of creativity and underutilized initiative.

Procrastination is also another problem associated with micromanagement as they delay delegation, holding on to work for too long. It contributes to leader overload, and the team receiving work too late to do it well.

There may be certain working environments where aspects of production or activity need to be managed closely, due to regulations, health and safety or performance standards. However, if you monitor the activity of others too closely and give them little control over what they are doing, you can quash enthusiasm and performance and also stop them from learning.

Micromanagement can lead to learned helplessness, and causes leaders frustration when others then do not take responsibility or ownership. This is often down to the team simply not being used to autonomy, which means they become overly dependent on the leader or they 'check out' through fear of criticism or apathy.

Leaders may presume that when decision-making powers are given to others, they may abuse that power or may be clumsy with the decisions they make. Yet the opposite is often true: they get the opportunity to show what they are made of.

Henry Stewart, founder of Happy, a learning and development company, thinks it's essential to give autonomy. Henry advises businesses on how to create happy and productive working environments, and he takes the same approach in his own company. He has very little involvement in decision-making, instead choosing to let the team do what they think is best. He has seen from experience that when you empower people and trust them, they will do a better job.

He gives 'pre-approval' so that people have the freedom to make decisions without worrying about whether it will be approved, and he has never objected to any idea. Sometimes things don't work out, but when that happens, people work things out themselves - it's all part of the process. Henry also gives people freedom over where and how they work and so unless someone is delivering training, he isn't worried about where they are. Henry attributes the company's success to the fact that the team has freedom, is listened to, feels valued and can work flexibly. They are autonomous. Interestingly, the only time that the company made a loss was when they tried to put more controls and monitoring in place.

New leaders can often fall into the trap of trying to control too much in a bid to keep performance stable. Yet remove the controls, and performance is often more likely to flow.

How to Build Autonomy

1. Agree what the outcomes need to be – leaders who provide a strong brief and a context for the work, and who focus on the outcomes, leave room for others to fill in the gaps and take ownership for the way in which they will achieve things.
2. Brief early – pass work on as soon as you can to avoid any delays and to give the team plenty of time to do a good job.
3. Understand there are different ways of doing things – just because someone hasn't done it the way you would have doesn't mean it's wrong, as long as they are achieving the outcomes that you agreed on at the start. It's important to allow the individual to put their own stamp on the work they do.

Leadership Myths

1. Leaders stay in control by monitoring all work.
2. Leaders need to govern the way people work.

Get Conscious

How much of your work is a) work you did before you were a leader, b) work which has become easy or straightforward for you, or c) work you are holding on to for fear of it 'not being done correctly'? Why are holding on to this work? Do you get frustrated that people haven't done work the way you would have done it? What would happen if you were to let go more? Do you ever feel as though the team isn't taking ownership? Is your behaviour creating that problem?

LESSON 7

Diversity Leads to Higher Performance

Diversity means including a range of things, people or ideas that may be different from each other. And in order to do that in a team setting, it means being open to difference. If we're honest, though, inclusion of difference makes things harder for a leader. Often it means disagreeableness in the team, longer timescales to get things done, and a conflict when it comes to recruiting people who fit but who are also different – that's a challenge.

To be inclusive as a leader, you need to genuinely believe that having a diverse range of people and ideas around you is better. Unfortunately, even though it's worthwhile in the longer term to create a team full of difference, people tend to be attracted to those who are similar to them and whose traits they admire.[36]

This isn't just at work – it plays out in our personal lives too. And if you're subconsciously scanning the horizon for people like you all of the time, you're missing the opportunity to connect with the people who are different, could complement your skills, and could challenge you on some of your own thinking, including limiting beliefs and assumptions. Often we don't like people who seem 'maverick' or different in their approach, yet often they're exactly who we need to boost performance or get us out of a hole.

The reality is that often leaders keep themselves safe and in control by limiting the amount of diversity around them. That may be one of the reasons we don't see much diversity at the top of organizations. When we surround ourselves with people we are used to working with and who are like us (or pretend to be), we are less challenged.

Maybe we like it that way, but that doesn't mean it's right for the organization. It can limit its progress.

When we look at gender diversity and ethnic diversity, for instance, we see they can positively impact financial performance in an organization by 15% and 35% respectively.[37]

It's the role of leaders to make everyone feel included, not just because this can generate better ideas and collaboration, but because of the impact that excluding people can have. We all crave social connection and are hardwired to be accepted as part of the group. This stems from our ancestors needing to be part of a group for survival and is something we carry with us to this day. When we are accepted, it helps us feel safe, and that has a positive impact on our mental health and the way we contribute in a group. By contrast, rejection and exclusion are bad for us – even if we just don't feel that we are part of or fit with the group. It can lead to all sorts of negative effects. People's sleep is affected, their immune system becomes stressed, and these effects can even lead to significant health issues. Depression, anxiety, aggression and low self-esteem can become a problem, because our bodies respond to rejection in the same way they react to physical pain. All of these effects can impact our performance at work.[38]

In the largest study of its kind on what leads to healthier and happier lives, Harvard researchers found that close relationships have the most powerful influence on our health. The study found that although taking care of our bodies is important, taking care of our relationships is a form of self-care and having strong social support leads to less mental deterioration.[39]

Every day, leaders make decisions about which of the team to invest in. Most of that is unconscious. Yet who are we leaving out if we're not diligent about making sure everyone feels included? We may not be naturally drawn to everyone we work with, but we have to be careful of our own perceptions and biases when it comes to leading a team. We don't have to be close to people all of the time, but we do have to be mindful that no one feels excluded. Often, through becoming more consciously aware of our biases or natural inclinations to spend time with certain people, we can adjust where we focus our time and effort in order to create more of a sense of unity and collaboration.

Inclusion is described as 'the act of including; the state of being included'[40] and in contrast, people can be excluded in many different ways:

- being left out of decisions when they should have been consulted
- being forgotten about when social events are organized
- leaders forming 'closer' relationships with some team members and not others
- being excluded because people don't like their ideas
- not being involved because they work flexibly or making it harder for people who are remote
- comments made that draw attention to someone in a negative way
- excluding someone from a project team without a robust and fair reason

Although in the real world it may not always be possible to include everyone, it is important to explain why they've been left out. Otherwise, people can reach unhelpful conclusions, which add to their feelings of exclusion.

To create inclusive cultures, leaders need to critically assess the way they operate. This will uncover ways of working that can be improved upon. Once leaders are committed to inclusion, and recognize how their own thinking and behaviour are having a daily impact, they become more consciously aware of what to change in themselves, and in the way the team works as a supportive group.

And it's OK to go on a journey with this; as a leader, you have to start with yourself, and your own values and behaviours, in order to be inclusive of others. That can take time.

How to Become a More Inclusive Leader
1. Encourage new thoughts – ideas and contributions from others. If you're not already doing this, it may not happen overnight, as people won't be used to it. Give it a chance, and over time people will trust that they can speak up.
2. Give everyone on the team time – regularly checking in with everyone to see how they're doing, balancing your time between team members.
3. Minimize hierarchy – understand that ideas can come from anywhere, and that everyone working together for the common good will achieve better results. Create opportunities for people at all levels inside and outside of the team to work more collaboratively together.

Leadership Myths
1. Inclusion means recruiting people from diverse backgrounds.
2. Like-minded people achieve the best results.

Get Conscious
How are you making people feel included? How do you get to know your people? What do you know about the people you work with? What adjustments have you made for those who work flexibly so that they still feel part of the group? Do you have any particularly close relationships with people in the team that could make others feel excluded? How do you encourage collaboration inside and outside of the team?

LESSON 8

See People as People and Not Objects

Very often, when leaders are under pressure to deliver at work, they see people around them as a means to an end, as resources to get work delivered, whether that be the people on their team, the suppliers who support them or their fellow leaders.

Seeing people as objects helps remove emotion and enables a more transactional, logical and efficient approach to team leadership.

Often what's getting in the way is any inclination to connect with people as people. You might remove the need for emotional engagement with others, especially the people who interest you less.

By connecting with the human (and not the object), you become curious and want to know more about people, their background, their family life, their passions, stresses and what drives them. Unless you know all of these things, how can you hope to understand where their true motivations lie and what may be getting in the way of them performing at their best at work? Unless you are emotionally connected to the team, what are the chances of them being emotionally connected to their work, and therefore inspired to accomplish what you need them to deliver? The chances are they won't be.

Think about an iceberg. We know that most of an iceberg is submerged below the waterline. What you can see isn't the full extent of what is going on. It's the same with people. Unless you ask people about themselves and become interested in them, you will never see what is really going on, the full extent of the person, and this creates a disconnect. Getting closer to people can feel awkward at times, especially early on in a relationship, and often we have to make a concerted effort as a leader to engage with people we wouldn't naturally be drawn to - not because we don't like them, but because there just isn't the same connection that we may have with others.

Often leaders can become frustrated that others aren't more like them, or that they don't 'get it'. Yet people are made of many unique experiences, values, beliefs, ways of working and ways of seeing the world, and this is bound to lead to differences of opinion, differences of approach and different ways of coping with the world around us.

Alain De Botton, the Swiss-born British philosopher, talks about what it is to be human and our many quirks and foibles. The School of Life that Alain founded runs conferences all over the world for people who are on a journey of self-actualization and who want to develop their emotional intelligence. I went to a conference in Zurich where Alain talked about knowing ourselves more, and how it allows us to watch for peculiar behaviour. As we're all a bit weird, but that being weird is normal. When we understand that, we are more compassionate with ourselves and with others. We're all just trying to be 'normal'.

In recognizing that, we see that we are all uniquely human, we all hurt, we've all experienced difficulties, we all have insecurities, and we all put on a facade in order to 'function' in everyday life. Most of us spend our time trying not to look like idiots, yet when we know that we're all trying to do the same thing, trying to put forward our best selves, it makes us feel better about being us. Seeing our own and other people's vulnerabilities brings us closer together, creating an emotional connection that gets below the surface of the iceberg.

If you see someone for all that they really are, every fibre that makes up their being, it can help you to see the human. Some people have had great childhoods, others haven't;

some have had great relationships, others haven't; some play the piano, while some people's parents couldn't afford music lessons; and some may have a religion, while others may be atheist ... and so on. It's the tapestry of our lives that affects who we are, how we behave and what we're good at, that often goes unnoticed. Through getting curious about who people really are, we build an emotional and deeper level of connection that makes each of us feel more worthwhile and more valued. That helps our wellbeing.

How to Make People Feel Like People

1. Get to know people – find out about their background, what they are interested in, what excites them, what annoys them, and their family, their hobbies, their frustrations. Explain those things about yourself too.
2. Stay connected – make the time to talk, to spend time together, to have fun, keep talking, and spend time inside and outside of work building a relationship.
3. Notice your avoidance tactics – there will always be people you're less inclined to speak to, even on your own team. Reflect on why you spend more time with certain people and not others. Make a conscious effort to open up opportunities for conversation with the people you'd normally be less inclined to connect with.

Leadership myths

1. You can be an effective leader without knowing your team.
2. People don't want you asking about their personal lives.

Get Conscious

Think about the fabric of your life – where did your greatest influences come from? If you see yourself as a puzzle, what would be in the picture? What might people be surprised to learn about you? What difficulties have you gone through in your life and how may they have influenced your current thinking and behaviour? Are you interested in finding out about other people? What stops you from asking people about their lives? Do you 'connect' with everyone in the team on the same level? What's getting in the way of you having better-quality relationships with your team?

LESSON 9

'Real Talk', Not Difficult Conversations

Having 'difficult' conversations is a normal part of work life. We often have conflicting views, need to discuss sensitive issues or have to broach subjects that we worry people will react badly to.

Yet starting off by viewing these conversations as difficult can make it harder from the outset. It's like standing at the foot of Mount Everest, looking up ahead of your ascent and thinking, "I'm not going to be able to do this." These thoughts will affect how easy your climb is. In order to get up the mountain, you need to feel positive about the challenge. Otherwise you'll feel anxious and see any setbacks as confirmation that you were going to fail. You may even give up.

Having a 'difficult' conversation is no different, and the way you frame a conversation is crucially important to its success. In other words, if you believe a conversation is going to be difficult, then it is more likely to be so. What you tell yourself about the conversation will influence how you approach it, how you feel and behave before and during the conversation, and how well you manage the message you're trying to convey. In other words, if you tell your brain it's going to be a bad, difficult or awful conversation, that will affect the way you 'show up' to that exchange. This is because our brains are wired to worry first and think second. Connections from the emotional systems to the cognitive systems are stronger than connections from the cognitive systems to the emotional system. To put it simply: when we're worried, emotions win and rational thought does not.[41]

What does that mean in practice?

Just imagine you are about to have a conversation about wanting a pay rise. You believe you work hard enough; you've had successes on your project throughout the year, and you have developed the team, so they are now achieving good results. All in all, it's been a good year. Yet on thinking about the conversation you're about to have with your boss, you imagine how they may respond to your request. You know they may say no, and you also know they are likely to point out your failings and the reasons why a pay raise is not possible. With all that in mind, you step into the room. You feel tense, you are ready to put forward a strong defence if they question your request, and you're already starting to villainize your boss and their short-sighted ways.

How do you think that will influence the way you turn up? The way you present your case? The way you respond when they ask you questions about your projects? You are likely to be defensive, and your reactions could end up inflaming the situation, rather than getting you what you want.

You were ready to have a difficult conversation, and so you end up having a more difficult one than was necessary. You needed to have a different starting point.

Usually when we enter a 'difficult' conversation it's because we need to discuss something important – either because we need to achieve something for ourselves, or because we need to point out something about someone else.

In an organization, it's necessary to create a culture where people can speak their mind, express honest opinions and say what they need to – anything else just gets in the way of performance. This type of open culture tends to lead to better results, and can be the spark needed for creativity and greater understanding of different perspectives. However, it means learning how to have 'difficult' conversations in a constructive way.

A concept I love, and which was introduced to me by Sean Ruane (see page 143), is the idea of 'real talk'. 'Real talk' is a necessary conversation, where emotions may run high, but one that is done with kindness and without judgement. The topic may still be difficult to tackle, but entering it with the best of intentions, and no judgment, makes it easier and takes out some of the negative emotion.

It's important to be able to have 'real talk' because often the short-term pain relief of leaving a topic undiscussed can lead to much bigger problems down the line.

When you consider that a conversation is going to be 'real talk' and not a difficult conversation, it changes your frame of mind, and when you learn how to have this type of conversation, it can open up opportunities for discussion about areas that you may never have felt you could raise, at work and at home.

How to Have an Effective Conversation

1. Get clear – about what you want the outcome of the 'real talk' to be and why you are having the conversation. 'Real talk' is having a conversation that will benefit someone else or you. It's an important conversation with a purpose. It should help, not hinder. You need to be clear about the intention – the intended outcome. And include facts. Make sure you've done your homework.

2. Don't be a victim – often when we go into a conversation like this, we're feeling emotional. As soon as we see these conversations as being about victims and villains, we often make ourselves right and others wrong which is unhelpful and doesn't take us closer to a solution. Seeing that there are two perspectives is important.

3. Listen – listen to what the other person has to say. Don't jump in; consider their perspective, ask them open questions to help them deepen their own understanding,

and allow the space for discussion. Even if you think you're right, there may be things you don't realize. Listening to hear, rather than to respond, will create the space for open dialogue.

Leadership Myths

1. You can't make a 'difficult' conversation comfortable.
2. Where opinions vary, you have to take control to get what you want.

Get Conscious

When you have to have a 'difficult' conversation, how often do you villainize the other person to make it easier to deliver the message? Are you open to hearing their perspective, or do you quickly become defensive or conciliatory? How much preparation do you do on the facts before having a conversation? Do you try to control the conversation to 'win' the battle? Do you go quiet and shut off from what the other person is saying? If so, how could you stay in the conversation constructively? Do you stay focused on the aim of the conversation or on winning?

LESSON 10

Stop Inducting People. Socialize Them

A feeling of togetherness can be created from the moment someone accepts a job. Yet, very often we hold out until day one of someone's job before building a relationship with a new employee, and sometimes we don't make enough effort at that point.

Organizations that recognize the importance of people try to help them to feel included from the start of their relationship – from when they accept the job. They don't wait until their first week to integrate them; they do it from the very start of the relationship. They don't see the induction as a formulaic and transactional procedure filled with protocols, policies and systems. They see it as a courting ritual where the individual is socialized into the culture, behaviour and character of the organization. It's a 'getting to know you' period, focused on ensuring the person feels included and good about the choice they've made. It's about building a relationship.

Often induction can be a functional 'tell' exercise that aims to convey information that will help the person find their way around, and find out what they are and are not allowed to do. Yet when a newcomer is seen as a source of energy that needs to be integrated into an even bigger source of energy, induction becomes something different. You see it as a process of socialization.

But why is this important? Isn't it simply acceptable to give them some policies, give them some tools to do their job, give them a space to work in and introduce them to some people they'll be working with? Why isn't that enough?

One reason is that having found them, you probably want to keep them. According to a US study, 31% of people quit their job within the first six months.[42] Another study showed that a third of people leave within three months.[43]

Although in some circumstances it was because the job wasn't what they expected, in many cases it was the on-boarding experience or culture that didn't match the individual's expectations.

The relationship an employee has with a new employer is no different to any other new relationship. The new job can look like an attractive prospect, but when the employee starts, they find that what attracted them in the first place was more of an illusion – and they are not attracted anymore. Unless organizations pay attention and make an effort during this initial courting phase of the relationship, they can fall at the first hurdle. Even if the person doesn't' leave, their productivity and engagement may be affected at an early stage. It can also impact their wellbeing.[44]

This is down to two key factors:

1. Dislocation of expectations – when an organization's selling points do not match a new employee's experience, they may feel a dislocation of expectation and lose faith in the new employer. Rather than focusing on getting started in the job, they spend their early weeks and months trying to work out whether the job or the environment was the right choice. This immediately and negatively impacts their performance and engagement.

2. The need to belong – when a new employee joins an organization, they want to feel accepted. They want to feel part of the team, trusted and able to contribute as quickly as possible. If they are not socialized into the behaviour of the 'tribe' and made to feel included, they may feel disconnected from the very group they've been recruited to be a part of.

Belonging is the feeling of being appreciated, respected and cared for as a team member. When people feel that they belong to a group, they share values, rituals and attitudes, and experience feelings of warmth and welcome that enrich their lives. Just imagine the person who turns up on their first day to be given the employee manual and new laptop, but who doesn't see their team leader for a day or two. How does that impact on their sense of belonging? How could that impact their ability to function effectively as part of the group?

An example of a company that does this well is Innocent Drinks; they work hard to make sure new starters feel included in the first two weeks of their employment. This is because the company recognizes the importance of socializing and of the awkwardness that people can feel when starting a new job. They get new employees involved in the various clubs they run – everything from gardening, to cheese and wine, to meditation – and they make sure they have someone to go to lunch with every day. And everyone's baby pictures go up on the wall to bring a bit of humour to the introduction of new family members. This contributes towards a more instant sense of belonging.

So find ways to share the culture of the organization, to show the personality of the people in it, to bring the team and what it does to life.

How to Socialize New Starters

1. Start early – find opportunities to connect with your new starter ahead of their first day by inviting them to team outings, to lunch or grab a coffee with them to get to know them more before they start.
2. Integrate them – by openly sharing as much as you can about the organization and how it behaves when the individual starts. Get as many people involved in their first few weeks as possible, invite them to meetings (internal and external), lunches and social gatherings,

and make sure that everyone is aware they are starting and makes them feel welcome. Use the early weeks to connect them to people, the team, other departments, providers, customers – the group they are going to be part of.

3. Focus on the positives – probationary periods are hugely counterproductive as they put too much focus on 'whether we like you' at a time when a new employee is already feeling vulnerable. If you're not willing to scrap the probationary period, make those few months an opportunity to agree what the person should focus on in their first few weeks and months and then give them feedback on where they are making a positive difference. Understand the individuals strengths and capabilities as much as possible and aim to build on these.

Leadership Myths

1. If someone has done the job before, they don't need an induction.
2. People will find their own way without being told about the culture.

Get Conscious

Do you celebrate when someone new has joined the team? Do you give them policies or socialize them into the team? Do you create opportunities to help them feel part of the group? Do you and others on the team take the time to explain how the culture works and how people work together? Do you create opportunities for the group to get together to get to know each other? Do you make them feel trusted from the start?

LESSON 11

People Need Flexibility

The Industrial Revolution started towards the end of the 18th century,[39] and it is amazing that to this day, we are still trying to figure out how to effectively combine our work and home lives.

Everyone wants to achieve a good balance between their work and home lives. What's more, no one wants to compromise their wellbeing for the sake of either of these things. Through greater flexibility, you can end up far more productive and engaged at work. Your mental and physical health is also likely to be better. Stress and burnout have been found to be lower among employees who have flexible working arrangements.[45]

Many employers still see the nine-to-five (if only it were nine-to-five) office-based working model as being relevant, expecting employees to come in to the office every day, leaving their home life neatly packed away in a box until the end of the day when they leave the office to open it up again. Even while at work, people's home lives still go on; they still have passions and interests outside of their jobs, they have family they need to care for. And some people just don't want to work in the same office all day – it just doesn't motivate them or keep them productive.

It's not just a case of providing flexibility on an ad hoc basis as and when people request it. It's about making flexibility a normal and accepted way of working. This means leaders shifting their mindset about how employees could work, rather than clinging to the idea that being present all day every day is the answer. There are plenty of organizations offering flexibility, but whether they are doing it in an effective way needs to be understood. According to one survey, 73% of employed people in the UK work either part time or full time with some form of flexibility offered.[46] Yet what's disappointing is that 30% of them feel that they are regarded as less important, with 25% given fewer opportunities than colleagues who worked conventional hours. A quarter also believe they had missed out on a promotion.

People shouldn't feel at a disadvantage for working part time or for having flexible hours. Often these people are still working full time – just in a different way.

Leaders who recognize that people have a life outside of work, who see the added stress that commuting in rush hour presents and who recognize that people want more control over how they work, create more collaborative, creative and healthy working environments. They allow people to manage their energy more effectively so that they do better work more often. They are also the ones who are likely to attract and retain the best people.

Flexibility, in all its forms, is becoming one of the most important benefits for employees. This means that organizations that don't provide it and support it will lose out in the long term. Often leaders struggle with the thought of giving people too much freedom, for fear that performance will drop or that the privileges will be abused. This parent/child dynamic, which lacks real trust, does nothing to enhance the employment relationship and wellbeing.

Ruth Gawthorpe of The Smart Working Revolution, a company that implements smart working in organizations, made a great point to me about this. Ruth rightly said that "work happens in brains and not offices." Although there will be situations where people have to be office-based, or where meetings or other activities mean they need to be with others, there are also as many situations when people do not need to be at their desks, or even in the office, to be productive.

A research study carried out with 20,000 people by the University of Birmingham Business School found that when people have a greater level of autonomy over hours, workplace, type of work or pace of work, those individuals' wellbeing was improved.[47]

Although it's not always possible to achieve complete flexibility (depending on the type of role), introducing it however and wherever possible is important. Flexibility will look different for different types of role, and not everyone in an organization will be able to work in the same way. It's about finding the flexibility that works, based on the type of team and the type of work. And then trusting people to make good choices. When we focus on outputs and not presenteeism, flexibility becomes so much easier to accept.

With so many organizations figuring out how to make this work, it will be those who don't pay attention to it who will lose productivity, good talent, and who will struggle to attract the best.

How Can You be More Flexible?

1. Give people options – there's a growing number of ways that people can work flexibly, from spending time in co-working spaces, to working from home, to having the ability to flex their hours. Get everyone involved in a discussion about what would work better for them. You'll need to work on the feasibility of the options and may want to trial options until you find what works for you.

2. Set boundaries – if everyone is able to come and go as they please without any guidelines, that could lead to confusion. Therefore, if there are certain meetings or events that people need to be available for, make that clear, and then people will know what to prioritize. Allow people flexibility around that to work in a way that suits them.

3. Focus on outputs – and not presenteeism, to measure how effective and productive people are. Agree what the overall outputs of work need to be and then give people the flexibility to figure out when and where they are going to do it. Leave the conversation open, so that if things don't work in the way you were both hoping, they can be tweaked.

Leadership Myths
1. People will work harder if they are at their desk.
2. If you give people control over their work, they will take advantage.

Get Conscious
Do you believe that the number of hours people work is a good measure of their performance? Where does that belief come from? Do you feel better when you have control over how and where you work? What stops you from trusting people to work in a way that suits them? Do you use task completion and presenteeism to measure performance? How could you focus more on outputs? Are you worried about what other leaders may think? Why don't you open up the conversation about flexibility at work?

LESSON 12

Space Affects the Way You Work

The workspace is evolving and with just 57% of employees around the globe agreeing that their workplaces enable them to work productively,[48] that's probably a good thing.

It's not a silver bullet, but space has a positive influence over collaboration, creativity and innovation. It also impacts productivity.

Leesman measures employee experience via the Leesman Index, a tool that captures employee feedback on how effectively the workplace supports them and their work. Through their extensive research, they've found that there are three categories of workplace:

1. Catalyst – the organization proactively shapes the way people work to support them in the best possible way and it leads to higher productivity.
2. Obstructer – employees have to jump over hurdles when trying to do their jobs, impacting their productivity.
3. Enabler – the employer 'makes work possible' but without actively pushing the boundaries.

This ability to define the approach that organizations take to the creation of workspace helps us understand the strategy we may wish to take when creating or using space that's more productive. It's not simply a case of providing a mediocre space and hoping for the best results.[49]

But what do people need? Although it's important to provide an environment that enables focused collaborative work and space for informal meetings, higher productivity is actually achieved when people have access to space for creative thinking, reading, and individual and focused work that is desk-based too. So, although collaborative space matters, individual space matters just as much.

As employers move toward more flexible and agile workplaces, it is impacting the space they use too. It means thinking about space in the most holistic sense – whether that be a fixed space, or any space where the employee feels productive. Many employers are finding that they can reduce the size of space they need and that the fixed space that is left over needs to be different. A good starting point in considering what space is needed is to look at the type of work employees do.

This may include calls, emails, critical thinking, creating, meetings, reading and so on. Not all work needs to be done in a fixed space and where it does, it doesn't have to be the office. Hence the significant growth of coworking spaces. Some organizations have even taken to walking meetings to get them outside more.

Space can also impact the culture you create. This is why architect Kerstin Sailer set up her company brainy-birdz to help employers think about office space and how it interfaces with the work culture. Historically, architecture has tended not to focus too much on the impact of buildings on social and psychological dynamics, but by paying attention to the impact that workplace design has on organizational culture, Kerstin has seen organizations achieve better results. Kerstin knows that building design is all about a compromise between planning, the history of the building, materials and the needs of the users. Yet despite potentially conflicting priorities, there is still a lot that can be done to create space that is both functional and that helps to create and promote a positive culture.

When the workplace is poorly designed and doesn't support the efforts of employees, it can suggest that the organization doesn't care much about its employees, and at worst it can show a scant regard, or even disrespect, for employee wellbeing.[50]

According to Ben Channon, an architect and chair of the Architects Mental Wellbeing Forum, we now spend more than 80% of our time in buildings, and this affects our mood both positively and negatively. Ben is passionate about improving mental health through how buildings are designed, and believes that designers have the opportunity to impact 'human' behaviour in a positive way.[51] Ben suggests that a small initial investment in the physical environment can have a big impact on productivity and retention rates – therefore adding a great deal of long-term value.

And when employers consider wellbeing in the design of space, they must also think about where employees go to reenergize. Havas Media, for instance, created a meditation lounge to give people time out, and breakout spaces or places where people can go to take a break, relax, play, or chat to friends are becoming increasingly important in the design of space. Having time for regular breaks not only meets your social need to connect, but also gives your brain a rest, and helps you to be more productive[52] and to be more efficient.[53]

How to Create Great Space

1. Assess activities – look at the activities that are carried out in your organization and the existing type of spaces. Do you have enough space for 'alone' work, for collaboration, for rest? Does the space create blockers to people being able to work in a number of ways?
2. Access flexibility – look at how free employees are to work in a way that suits them. Are people allowed away from their desks? Do you allow time out for thought and creativity? How free are people to move around the space

and to work outside of the office? Do all leaders give people the same levels of freedom?

3. Access the conditions – look at the standards that define what good working space looks like. There are a number of great resources out there, like Neil Usher's book, *The Elemental Workplace*. Get feedback from the team about how productive the space is. Make big changes if you can, or small changes if you can't.

Leadership Myths

1. People do their best work at their desk.
2. Collaborative space is most important to employees.

Get Conscious

Have you given much thought to the impact of space on the team? Do you understand the different types of work they do? Do you understand how you do your best work – in what space? Do you give your team the flexibility to work where they want to? Do you take regular breaks? Do you encourage others to do the same? Do you afford others the same flexibility you have yourself?

CASE STUDY

Building Togetherness
with GRAHAM

Situation

GRAHAM is a privately owned construction, facilities management and investment company. They hold Platinum accreditation with Investors in People as well as having proudly gained their Investors in People Health & Wellbeing award in 2017. In 2018 they were placed 16th in the *Sunday Times* Grant Thornton Top Track 250 list with an annual turnover of £735m. The construction industry is known for being a challenging environment to work in, which is why Executive Chairman Michael Graham decided that wellbeing needed to be at the top of the people agenda. His vision was to become a 'Leader for Wellbeing' within the industry.

Problem

Construction is a male-dominated industry, a group traditionally reluctant to seek health advice. Individuals tend to make poor health choices, and this impacts absence levels and subsequently project delivery. On the positive side, a healthy employee will be engaged and more productive, so GRAHAM recognized the business benefit of supporting and investing in the health of their people.

Solution

GRAHAM's leadership team had long valued these business benefits of wellbeing and, in 2013, they set about cascading the principles of their wellbeing strategy. They focused on what they called Whole Person Development, maximizing individual engagement and productivity through giving employees the right skills and resilience to do their job, while ensuring they were at the optimum level of physical and mental health. Investors in People was later engaged to ensure an independent assessment of 'Wellbeing' processes and provide challenging targets to aspire to.

One of the first things GRAHAM wanted to make sure was that managers felt more comfortable supporting employees with their wellbeing, so they brought in specialists to train managers to communicate effectively with individual employees and coach them to manage their own wellbeing. They also used a diagnostic tool to assess what an employee had to change and how 'well' employees were at meeting the wellbeing targets they had set for themselves.

To support physical health, group-wide, regional team activities and events were launched, including an Around the World in 80 Days Step Challenge, marathon sponsorship and regional cycling groups. They also supported people with weight management and offered voluntary mini health checks for all staff.

Communication was key to getting employees involved and as well as a wellbeing anchor video delivered by Michael Graham setting out the company vision and strategy for wellbeing, various other communications helped to bring the topic to life. These included a focus on National Campaigns, a wellbeing calendar of information and events, positive news stories about wellbeing posted through the intranet and email blasts, along with wellbeing talks, information boards and a designated Twitter feed @grahamwellbeing.

GRAHAM invested heavily in making it work, putting in place a governance group, a functional delivery team and a channel that enabled employees to put forward their ideas for change, which GRAHAM then acted on. Investors in People was asked to help structure that journey, monitoring progress and setting new challenges. Progress was regularly reviewed by collecting wellbeing data, such as weight management, alcohol consumption and take up of activities. This was piloted and best practice was rolled out to all employees, agreeing on an annual plan, monitoring progress, and by incorporating wellbeing into site and business risk assessments.

Impact

Employees responded well and enjoyed being able to take on physical challenges with their colleagues, helping to improve the isolation people often experienced working and living away from home. The positive impacts didn't end there:

- Absences reduced by 100% in the last two years
- Staff turnover reduced by 33%
- Staff engagement increased by 20% over the last two years
- 90% of people gave positive feedback on the wellbeing programme
- 20% reduction in the number of smokers
- Sign-up to 'wellbeing' activities increased by 50%

What Next?

GRAHAM has made good progress, but they are not stopping there. Key to the future success of wellbeing at GRAHAM will be the 'personalization' of support for each individual through its wellbeing programme CONNECT where wellbeing experts provide a wellbeing diagnostic tool, a personal plan and coaching for all employees. GRAHAM intends to continue their journey in collaboration with Investors in People and have supported collaborative learning by speaking to other organizations at a number of events.

"People don't just join businesses for money or career development. These may be the important starting points, but the type of employer you are is what keeps people in the long term. If you value individuals and have a focus on wellbeing, people respond. They want to be with your company and will encourage and attract others, leading to a pipeline of success."

Michael Smyth
HR Director, GRAHAM

CASE STUDY

Working in Partnership
with Make Architects

Situation

Ken Shuttleworth, the founder of Make Architects, wanted to create a different kind of architecture firm. Coming from an industry of 'maestro' architects, where having your name on the building you designed was important, Ken's vision was to create a firm where credit was shared, and where everyone involved could have a say and influence over what the company did. He wanted to avoid one person taking all the credit for what was, in reality, a team effort.

Ken's family values drove his approach, ensuring no one should be overlooked. His architectural passion for 'creating environments to improve people's lives' was to be central to Make's ethos – for clients, and the people who work at Make.

Challenge

Ken wanted to create an environment where everyone was able to put forward great ideas without fear of failure or criticism. If your idea was used, you'd get the credit.

He also wanted to make sure that regardless of whether a particular project was making money or not, the profits would be shared – because everyone was working equally hard. His aim was to create a 'grown-up' environment where intelligent people could take responsibility for making a real difference.

Solution

This is what led Ken to set up an 'employee-owned' company, with all shares held in trust - the 'purist' model of employee ownership, according to Ken. It meant all employees effectively own the company, so it can't be sold without everyone's agreement. It gives everyone a say about how the company is run, and the financials are totally transparent - a single company-wide cost centre that everyone has a role in contributing to.

He also wanted to make the office a vibrant place to work. Rather than being out on a business park, he wanted a central location, where people could go home in the evening, feeling better than they did when they arrived in the morning. So, he created a modern, open plan space, where people were surrounded by amenities and the buildings that they were part of creating. And the projects were exciting, too.

Ken believes that everyone needs to feel included, regardless of whether they are an architect or someone working in HR, PR or finance. So, these non-architectural functions became 'core staff' as the 'backbone of the office'. Importantly, there is also no obvious hierarchy – everyone is called a 'partner', and there are no other job titles to differentiate members of the team.

As the company evolved, the partners (or 'Makers', as they call themselves) came up with more ways of creating an inclusive culture. 'Friday Live' became the platform for anyone to talk about what they were working on and share ideas, and speakers were invited to expand knowledge-sharing and provide inspiration. They also created a Make Forum, which Makers volunteer to be part of. This group facilitates discussion on ways to improve the studio and working environment, and people from all areas of the practice can be part of it. Similarly, the team recognized that only through having a diverse range of recruiters would they end up with a diverse range of talent, so partners from various levels across the business contribute to the recruitment process.

When it comes to expenditures, everyone takes ownership to make sure that spending is sensible, so there's no expensive furniture or first-class travel; the 'frills' are lost in favour of sharing in the profits at the end of the year. It also leads to a more collective effort when it comes to cost cutting, with everyone working together on money-saving initiatives.

A strong ethos has evolved at Make to 'treat people well' and to see 'everyone as equal', setting the tone for a culture of togetherness: a largely self-organized system where 'everyone can do everything' – if they want to take on the challenge. This is how they continue to unlock people's potential through removing any barriers to people being able to use their best skills and ideas. Although generally the most experienced people take the lead, there is less of a power struggle.

Outcome

This way of working seems to make a positive difference in the way employees feel about their work lives. They feel empowered, trusted and supported. And although (like in any business) there are sometimes problems, on the whole people seem pretty happy.

Make wants to continue to improve, and something it is currently considering is how to give people a sense of identity where there is no real hierarchy or job titles. Some people can struggle with not being able to define a clear role when dealing with clients, and sometimes people want greater clarity about how they are progressing in comparison to their peers.

Make has been phenomenally successful over the years, and its culture is certainly a contributing factor to that – the transparency, the lack of ego, the way everyone is motivated to work for the collective good, the responsibility everyone has without worrying about getting things wrong. People are allowed to evolve ideas without fear of reprisal.

The social connection also seems to be an important part of the culture of 'togetherness', with one partner explaining that "if you make friends and build social connections and shared experiences, it helps you to get through the tough times".

TOGETHER

A Little Recap

In order to do their best work, people need social connections and to feel safe at work – they also need the right space to work in. Breaking down the hierarchy, creating a sense of togetherness and giving freedom allows people to express themselves more authentically, to work better as a team, and to take ownership for their contribution and how they work. This all leads to better performance and wellbeing. Here's a recap on what was covered in this section:

1. Leaders need to stay away from command-and-control leadership and **work in partnership with people** to build better-quality relationships and results.
2. **Leaders are enablers** who are there to bring out the best ideas in others. Through providing guidance, coaching and connecting people together, leaders leverage the potential around them.
3. **You need to feel safe** to express yourself, to admit to mistakes and to open yourself up to new learning, all of which can positively impact your performance and wellbeing.
4. **Leaders are adults, not parents**, and through creating adult-to-adult relationships, and having better quality conversations and relationships, leaders enable better results.
5. **Great leaders embrace failure** because they understand that it's only through trial and error and through being tolerant of performance dips that the best results will be achieved.

6. People want **autonomy at work**, as it allows them the freedom and flexibility to make decisions about how they work and where to focus. When employees are empowered, they take on more responsibility and deliver better results, as they feel valued and appreciated.

7. **Diversity leads to higher performance**. Through creating a diverse environment of people who have varying experiences and perspectives, the most creative, innovative and well-rounded ideas can be developed.

8. People's uniqueness can often be overlooked, and that lack of insight leads to them being treated in a way that is unproductive. When **people are seen as people and not objects**, it creates a deeper understanding and connection that leads to better outcomes.

9. Important conversations at work are often dealt with in a clumsy way. When challenging conversations are seen as **'real talk' and not difficult**, it sets up the right framework through which to have a better-quality conversation.

10. Stop seeing the early days of employment as functional and transactional. By **socializing people instead of inducting them**, you recognize the importance of bringing them into the group, giving them a sense of belonging, and sharing the values and behaviours of the organization from the earliest stage.

11. **Employees need flexibility** to blend work and home life and to capitalize on their unique working styles. Trusting employees is the starting point for flexibility.

12. Consider the types of work employees do, their need for individual and collaborative space, and whether they always need to be in a fixed space to do the best job. **Space affects the way you work**, which is why the intentional creation of effective workspace is an important factor in building productive and healthy workplaces.

RESILIENT

Life Will Throw
You Lemons

The Big Conscious Question: What Mindset Do I Need?

Resilience in the workplace has never been so important. We're facing an unprecedented time, both economically and societally, with change and uncertainty in abundance. Without resilience, we will find it hard to navigate. Both at an organizational and individual level, resilience gives us the strength and perspective to better deal with the inevitabilities of life.

Now, it's important to be clear about what resilience is not. It is not an expectation that you will stay strong regardless of the pressures, the workload, the crises and the tragedies that you experience. No. Resilience is about bouncing back. Realistically, unless you've reached a stage of enlightenment reserved for the likes of Gandhi and the Dalai Lama, you are likely to be affected by the difficulties experienced in life. What resilience will provide you with is the ability to recover more quickly from setbacks.

Imagine the employee who is taken through a redundancy consultation process due to a team restructure. Their job is put at risk, and following consultation, they end up keeping their job. The process takes four weeks. During that time, the employee has no idea if they will have a job at the end of the process; they know that the job market is tough, and that financially, the family will be in trouble if they are not earning two incomes. That is going to cause anxiety. The point isn't whether anxiety is experienced, but how intense it is, how much it affects functioning and how long it takes to recover from. Expecting anyone to be totally unaffected by the dramas of life is unrealistic, but with resilience you can cope better.

Without that resilience, the process of a redundancy consultation could end up being debilitating, leading to unhealthy stress levels and encouraging the individual to believe in worst-case scenarios. This can also affect the recovery process, and may affect productivity, mental health and even relationships – both inside and outside of work. So there is a lot to be gained from building greater resilience. The crucial differentiators to someone with resilience, in contrast to someone without it, are their mindset and self-management.

Some people are more naturally resilient, and the older generation in particular is generally better skilled at self-management than younger folk.[54] And although age can give you the wisdom to view the trials and tribulations of life in a more productive and positive way, you don't have to wait until you are old to develop these skills. Through becoming more consciously aware of your reactions and mindset, you can build your resilience.

Resilience fluctuates based on life circumstances. Being resilient enough to deal with one challenge can be straightforward, but it is more difficult when one is facing numerous pressures. And we're all different, so what one individual may struggle with, someone else may find unproblematic.

Life will throw you lemons, we know that for sure. It's your ability to get used to eating them that will lead to greater resilience, and therefore greater wellbeing and performance.

This section of the book will help you understand what leads to greater resilience, what you need to do to better look after yourself, and how to remove some of the barriers you may have created that are getting in the way of your own resilience.

LESSON 13

Everyone Is Fine ...
Yet Your Mental Health Is Failing

Many people think that when we talk about mental health, we mean mental illness. This is not the case. We all have mental health, in the same way we have physical health. They are both crucial components of our overall wellbeing.

Mental health has been a taboo topic for some time, but is now becoming more of a mainstream subject, which is in no small part down to the poor state of the nation's mental health. One in three British workers each year experiences a mental health problem, and poor mental health is the leading cause of sickness absence, with one in five 'highly engaged' employees at risk of burnout.

The consequences of poor mental health are often not visible, so most of the time we just presume people are 'fine'. And although awareness has grown it's still a hugely stigmatized area. David Beeney, a passionate ambassador for mental health and founder of Breaking the Silence, is helping employers better understand mental health. He believes that the meaning of the word 'mental', which is perceived negatively (not out of spite, but ignorance), doesn't help in breaking down the stigma around mental health. And unless we view mental health in the same way we see physical health, as something that needs exercise and nourishment, it will continue to be stigmatized.

And it starts in childhood. In a modern world where there's more choice, more uncertainty and more risk – all driven by advances in technology – children and young people suffer too. We're all human, just at different stages of our journey. Children and young people need to be equipped with the tools to navigate modern life to reduce the risk of mental health issues developing in adulthood. This is why Clare Pass and Rachael Bushby from Dragonfly: Impact Education set up their business. As former teachers themselves, they recognized the need to give younger folk help earlier in their development,due to the increasing pressures they face nowadays.

Although mental health is a broader topic and is as much about staying mentally well as dealing with mental illness, employees still don't feel they can be open about their mental health problems, with one in five feeling they can't tell their boss about being overly stressed at work. Although stress in itself isn't a mental health problem, it can lead to one. Less than half of people diagnosed with a mental health problem are sharing this with their manager.[55] Many people would agree that it is much easier taking time off work because of a broken leg or other physical health problem than explaining that they're experiencing anxiety or depression due to the potential repercussions of disclosing such personal information.

Pressure and some level of stress is good, as we need a certain amount to perform, and stress is a normal part of daily life. It's when it becomes too much, or when we've suffered for too long, that it becomes a problem. In the UK, employees are taking 70 million work days off a year to deal with their mental health problems,[56] and poor mental health is costing employers between £33 billion and £42 billion per annum.[57]

This stems from presenteeism, where individuals are at work but are significantly less productive due to poor mental health, as well as sickness absence and employee turnover. And what's even more worrying is that 300,000 people with a long-term mental health problem lose their jobs each year.[58] Emma Mamo from Mind, the mental health charity, explained that their Workplace Wellbeing Index for 2017/18 showed that over 73% of employees have experienced poor mental health in their current job.

This is just one of the reasons that Mind is encouraging employers to develop better strategies for supporting the mental health of their employees. They believe that employers should clearly set out how the organization supports staff with mental health problems, and the options available should they become unwell. This also means having policies and procedures that promote wellbeing and tackle the work-related causes of poor mental health.

James Routledge, founder of Sanctus, a company providing mental health coaches to organizations, is keen for people to recognize that mental ill health is only one end of the mental health spectrum. Even if you're feeling seven or eight out of ten, having the opportunity to speak to someone can really help to improve your mood and focus your performance. Through creating a safe space for people to talk openly, it can relieve the day-to-day pressures and challenges that most people face.

It's not just employers who can take steps, though. You often don't see that your own mental health isn't where it should be. You can see a cut or bruise, but noticing red flags when it comes to mental health, especially when you're in the thick of things, can be hard. The most common mental health illnesses are anxiety and depression, and most people will experience them at some point in their lives. It's important to recognize the symptoms:

- feeling anxious and irritable
- feeling down
- finding it difficult to concentrate
- having problems sleeping
- changes in mood
- feeling teary
- feeling paranoid

Panic attacks, a racing heart or tightening chest can also mean that something's not right, and sometimes things are even more serious, with people experiencing suicidal thoughts, having problems managing money, or depending on alcohol or drugs to feel better.[60]

These problems are a normal part of life, but when they go 'underground', they can become much worse. They can lead to people becoming withdrawn, isolated and feeling overwhelmed. It's often people in senior roles or high performers who have the biggest surprise when they discover they have a mental health problem. Due to the pressure they're often under, it's only a matter of time before something snaps.

Mental ill health is normally not permanent - it can be managed and improved. In the same way as someone makes a full recovery from a broken leg, the same is true of anxiety or depression.

And given that the return on investment can be significant for employers who invest in workplace health initiatives, there is commercial gain to taking employee wellbeing and mental health education and support more seriously.[61]

How to Better Your Mental Health

1. Open up – the starting point is to talk about it, remove the stigma and educate yourself and others about the signs, so that people pick up on problems earlier. Openness starts with leaders, as showing vulnerability allows others to do the same.
2. Educate yourself – read up on mental health, find out more about it, organize or go to a talk or workshop. There are lots of resources out there now through your doctor, and organizations like Mind, Public Health England, Business in the Community and the World Health Organization.

3. Get help – this is often the biggest problem, especially for leaders. Speaking to your doctor, a psychotherapist, a coach, a close family member, a partner or a friend can help you make sense of what you're experiencing. Often the pressure of holding on to the way you feel makes matters worse.

Leadership Myths

1. People who suffer with mental health problems are weak.
2. If you suppress your anxiety, it will go away.

Get Conscious

How honest are you with yourself about how you're feeling? Can you spot any signs that you are under too much pressure? Has your behaviour been erratic lately? Are you behaving 'well' around others? Do you use any copying mechanisms to deal with the stress you are facing, such as drinking, smoking, overeating etc.? Have you opened up about the way you are feeling? What is stopping you from seeking help?

LESSON 14

Put Your Own Oxygen Mask On

For some reason, we struggle to make decisions in the here and now that will lead to better health outcomes in the future. In many ways, we can be pretty sensible. We pay into life assurance policies in case we die early, some of us pay into pensions so we can maintain our standard of living in the future, and we do DIY on our homes to make sure we keep a roof over our heads.

Yet when it comes to personal health, we are often remiss. We know that exercise, nutritious food and hydration are good, and that smoking, alcohol, sugar and junk food are bad. And even though we know some of these things can lead to debilitating health conditions, and even death, most of us carry on regardless. We seem to be able to picture a future without money and don't like the way that looks, but an image of our health deteriorating seems harder to create.

In our busy lives, there is so much going on that consuming unhealthy food and drink, and missing out on exercise, are almost like rewards for our hard work. Stress doesn't help, as we are more likely to indulge in addictive behaviour, such as drinking and smoking, when we are stressed. The stress hormone cortisol is also a factor: its levels surge to provide energy to cope in stressful situations, but too much cortisol can have crippling effects.[62]

Stress is bad for us. We make bad lifestyle choices because of stress, and the way it manifests in our bodies makes us sick in the long term. It can lead to us suffering from headaches, sleep problems, weight gain, digestive problems, memory problems and even heart attacks.[63]

In New York, Los Angeles and other municipalities, the relationship between job stress and heart attacks is well acknowledged. For instance, a police officer who suffers a coronary event, on or off the job, is assumed to have a work-related injury and is compensated accordingly.[64]

One of the most startling books I've read on this subject is Jeffrey Pfeffer's *Dying for a Paycheck*. Pfeffer has done extensive research demonstrating that "people are literally dying for a paycheck". He points out that although companies obsess over their carbon footprint, they would do well to consider the 'footprint' they are leaving on the human beings they employ – another carbon-based life form. His point is stark. Over the years, companies have been paying more attention to their corporate responsibilities, to the point where, in many cases, the balance has swung in favour of the world outside of the organization. They are saving the planet while killing their people. A double standard, maybe?[65]

It's not that global problems aren't important – we need a planet to live on – but if we don't look after ourselves, our time on it will be short-lived.

Leaders have a responsibility to figure out how to fix this not just for their own sakes, but for the sake of the people they lead. It's the right thing to do morally, but it also makes commercial sense, as employees who are less stressed and who feel well perform better.[66]

So, what leads to stress? Well, there are many causes of stress, but some of these are:
- heavy workloads
- long hours
- not being able to use your skills
- lack of inclusion in decision-making
- poor communication
- poor work-life balance
- lack of support or help
- conflicting or uncertain job expectations
- too much responsibility
- job insecurity

- lack of opportunity
- rapid changes for which people are unprepared
- unpleasant or dangerous working conditions
- being treated differently than others
- physical or verbal abuse[67]

All of these can contribute to poor mental health and are a good starting point when assessing areas for improvement in the organization. The positive news about stress and mental health, more generally, is that organizations can make changes that have a positive impact, through addressing some of the ways in which they operate.

Leaders need to lead the way and role model good behaviour when it comes to good mental health. If the leaders in the organization aren't well and don't role model healthy behaviour, it makes it very hard for everyone else to look after themselves. For instance, a leader who works long hours and who rarely switches off makes it harder for their team to do the same – I know, that was me. Whether that's because they send emails out of work hours, never leave the office on time, or create unrealistic workloads, their behaviour will have a knock-on effect. Leaders must first 'put on their own oxygen mask' before they can take proper care of others.

And it's not just day-to-day organizational behaviours that help. Employees can be empowered too. Katrina Stamp from Flock, a marketing transformation company, told me how they are better supporting the mental health of their employees by giving everyone a pot of money to spend on wellbeing and development. This has led to people being able to fund their Pilates, yoga, massage classes and gym memberships. It's this combination of investment in our wellbeing as well as changing some of our own behaviours, that we can build our resilience to cope – and take care of our wellbeing long term.

How to Manage Stress

1. Take an honest look at the list of causes of stress (above), and decide which of these are impacting on your life. How are you really feeling? Where does your stress come from?
2. Critically assess and review the way you work – is it healthy? Often you may not see that you're not working effectively, and that you're taking long-term risks with your health. Are you nourishing yourself with breaks, good food, exercise, social time and so on? Or are your habits more inclined to damage your health with over-work, limited down time or alcohol, for example?
3. Take better care of yourself – decide on one or two lifestyle and work changes that will have a positive difference on your health. Decide why you are making the change, what you want the outcome to be and plan how to make that change. Then start making the improvements. And don't beat yourself up about the odd bad day.

Leadership Myths

1. Stress won't affect my long-term health.
2. I've always worked this way, so I'll be fine.

Get Conscious

Do you feel OK? How are your stress levels? Can you think of a time when you didn't feel stressed? What is leading to the way you feel? Can you focus properly? What do you do for yourself? What makes you feel well? What's stopping you from including more of those 'well' activities in your diary? Are you using coping mechanisms to avoid/deal with the problem? Are you setting a good example for the people around you?

LESSON 15

Brain Health Matters

The brain is our operating system, but it's funny how most people don't have a clue about how it works. And that's not all – when it doesn't seem to be working quite right, we tend not to know how or who to ask for help.

There aren't many operating systems in the world where the user, the super-user in this case, has little comprehension of how the system works. We're constantly using our brain, but at no point do we get taught about how it works, how to look after it and how to optimize its effectiveness. Just imagine a car that is never serviced, a plane that is never checked for glitches, or a database that is never cleansed, and then not having the user manual to figure out what's wrong when any of them fail.

Your brain is all you have – it's behind everything we think, feel and do. So, looking after your mental health is crucial if you want to achieve the best outcomes. Neuroscience has come a long way in the last couple of decades, and we now have a much better understanding of what we can do to keep our brains healthy and high-functioning. By understanding what causes the brain stress or anxiety, what depletes mental energy and what restores it, you can remove some of the causes of stress, learn how to focus better, and take greater control over how you feel and 'operate'.

The brain is incredibly complex and there is no need to understand it all. However, there are two areas that I have found particularly interesting.

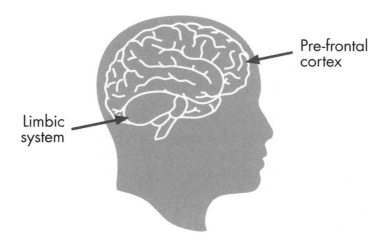

The first is the prefrontal cortex (PFC). This is often referred to as the CEO, or the 'Executive Centre', of the brain, and it is responsible for much of our higher-level cognitive function, including attention and processing. It's the part of our brain that stops us from swearing at an inopportune moment (helping our self-control) and it helps us to plan and make decisions. It helps us focus on our goals and it is also involved in delaying gratification, which is important in helping us achieve our goals.

When under stress, tired or overwhelmed, the PFC doesn't perform as well, which can lead to us feeling uninspired, focused on negative thoughts, or being overly emotional and forgetful. When it's working well, it helps with creativity and attention, and boosts working memory, which enables us to plan and focus better. It also means we stay more in control of our emotions – we're better regulated.

The second brain area that everyone should know about is the limbic system. This area is partly responsible for dealing with emotions. It houses the amygdala, which processes our emotional responses, memory, attention and the ability to focus on some things to the exclusion of others. It's heavily involved in identifying fear and is responsible for the 'fight-or-flight' response, as its aim is to protect us. The limbic system is connected to the PFC, so if the amygdala becomes unsettled, so does the PFC. That's what impacts our performance and our ability to think straight.

Psychologist Daniel Goleman coined the term 'amygdala hijack' to explain what happens when our amygdala is triggered by a threatening situation. If the amygdala senses danger (perceived or real), it makes a split-second decision and begins the fight-or-flight response before the prefrontal cortex has time to overrule it.[68] This all happens in a flurry and normally without conscious awareness. Through a better understanding of what triggers you, or what is likely to, you can take greater control over this subconscious response, which can often take hours or longer to recover from. Also, by recognizing that our emotions affect our ability to focus, we can make better choices about when we work and in what way.

How Can I Look after My Brain?

1. Look after your prefrontal cortex – prioritize what you need to focus on, remove distractions, be intentional with how you organize yourself, reward yourself for making progress towards goals, and become more mindful (see Lesson 21: Moving to a More Mindful World).

2. Keep your amygdala calm – it's important to get enough sleep and manage your stress levels. Relationships can help with the function of the amygdala because trust is important in maintaining a good balance. Meditating has been found to reduce activation in the amygdala, helping with emotional regulation. Taking a few long, deeps breaths, before or during a situation that triggers stress and anxiety, can reduce activity in your amygdala, so that you can get back in control.

3. Take care of your brain – there are numerous ways to take care of your brain and help it function more effectively:
   - Make sure you're eating well and staying hydrated
   - Laugh – it is a great de-stressor
   - Challenge the brain through learning and doing new things
   - Let the mind wander, enabling 'aha!' moments to flow
   - Exercise to get the blood flowing to the brain
   - Plan your day and think about what work needs to be done and when
   - Stick to one task at a time. Multitasking requires you to move your attention quickly from one thing to another, which can be tiring for the brain
   - Take short breaks. Making the brain work nonstop isn't effective and doesn't lead to best thinking

Leadership Myths
1. I can't do anything about my emotional reactions.
2. Working hard keeps the brain working well.

Get Conscious
Are you able to stay focused on what you're doing? Do you have uncontrolled emotional reactions? How well are you looking after your brain health? Have you tried mindful meditation? Do you drink enough water? Do you allow yourself to have breaks?

LESSON 16

Befriend Ambiguity

Too much uncertainty can impact your ability to stay resilient, yet with so much change and ambiguity in the workplace, a degree of uncertainty is a normal part of working life. The problem is that the human brain is still programmed with primal instincts, and any uncertainty or ambiguity can trigger the fight-or-flight response, as it would have back in primitive times if that brain was faced with a sabre-toothed tiger. We also make lots of assumptions, so when we don't know what is happening or when there is a gap in our knowledge, we either consciously or subconsciously try to fill it.

The brain is constantly trying to conserve energy, and in order to function well, it creates habits and shortcuts and makes predictions and assumptions about what is going to happen. According to Hilary Scarlett, author of *Neuroscience for Organizational Change*, the goal of our brain is survival, and it is constantly trying to make predictions so it can keep us out of harm's way by avoiding threats and seeking rewards. The problem is that the threat response is much stronger.[69] So, when we feel we may be under threat, which often happens when we are not in control or don't have all the information, our brains get anxious.

That can lead to a loss of focus, increased stress levels, sleepless nights and negative thinking, which affect our mood and behaviour.

Generally speaking, unless you have been trained to deal with ambiguity, or have the emotional bandwidth and regulation to manage it, and unless you feel like you have a grip on what is happening around you, ambiguity can be stressful.

And becoming 'emotional' can affect our ability to make good decisions. It can also leave us ruminating about threats or possible outcomes that don't exist – this is clearly a waste of energy. The immune system can also be affected by increased levels of cortisol (the stress hormone) and depleted dopamine levels (the happy hormone).[70]

That feeling of 'not knowing' can really mess us up, and when it comes to our performance at work, it can have a detrimental impact. This is one of the reasons why for years, leaders have been told about the importance of communication. It's because leaders have a key part to play in employees knowing what is going on – thus minimizing the risk of uncertainty. Leaders who are open and honest, and who keep people updated, are more likely to lessen stress in the workplace and keep people focused on what matters: doing a great job.

When employees become distracted, worrying about what may or may not be about to happen – because they are filling gaps – it can affect their wellbeing and their performance. So, leaders who regularly communicate are better leaders.

We won't always be able to find out what's happening, though, and we certainly won't predict all the work and personal events that lie ahead. That's why getting comfortable with a certain level of uncertainty and change is important, because this makes us more resilient.

Although we won't always be able to fight our natural instinctive reactions, especially where we feel highly threatened and we are dealing with a number of stressors, we can get better at managing our reactions and perceptions of many day-to-day situations that could leave us feeling uncertain. This ability will help you focus your performance and protect your mental health.

How to Befriend Ambiguity

1. Don't make up stories – humans are very good at creating stories in their own minds, often based on scant or no factual data. We can quickly create a version of reality, a 'story' fuelled by our fears that bears little or no relation to what is actually going to happen. Our anxiety levels soar, and we end up fixated on what might be. It's important to stay grounded in fact and reality.

2. Recognize what's happening in your brain – simply knowing more about your threat responses can help you manage your reactions more effectively. And by becoming more aware of your natural inclination to react badly to threats, you will better understand why you feel the way you do when you are threatened. This conscious awareness can also help you take more control over your mental state.

3. Ask why you're threatened – often we're not consciously aware of why we're feeling worried or stressed about something. We have a subconscious fear that is triggered by uncertainty, and we start to feel bad, not realizing why. Our body is often the first thing to react. When something is making you feel uncomfortable, reflect on why that might be. By bringing some options into your conscious awareness, you can more rationally decipher what may be going on, in order to take control of your reactions.

Leadership Myths

1. I won't feel better until I know what is happening.
2. The stories we tell ourselves are normally true.

Get Conscious

How good are you at dealing with change? What is it about the uncertainty that unsettles you? Do you tend to think about worst-case scenarios? How could you be more positive about the changes or uncertainty that you experience? Do you allow yourself to be influenced by others who are negative? Do you keep others updated with progress, even if you don't know the answers?

LESSON 17

Carefully Choose Your Frames

The way we view a situation, and therefore the meaning we apply to it, is referred to as 'framing'. The frame we apply to a situation affects the way we respond to it.

Take, for instance, when you find out that someone new is joining the team. It's a senior person and you will be reporting to them. You weren't expecting it, and you are bit shocked. You start to process the news and make sense of it. This is where you choose your frame (normally a subconscious process) and the way you are going to interpret the change.

Everyone perceives things differently, and you can never expect one person to react in the same way as others. This is because we receive information in different ways and interpret it based on our unique life experiences and memories, beliefs and values. The language used to deliver the message, and the time and space we are in when we receive it, also make a difference.

When new information is received, our brain tries to process and make sense of it quickly, and sometimes data is distorted, generalized or deleted during the process. The way we internally represent the data can affect our state of mind, physiology and behaviour. It's the mental shortcuts that we use to speed up our reasoning that can make us consistently irrational about and sensitive to how things are framed.[71]

Yet we have more influence over our responses than we think. Choosing the right frame can have a positive impact on the way we feel, and the wrong frame can debilitate us and impact our resilience and ability to cope. By becoming more conscious of our reactions, and realizing that they are often based on past experiences and not what we're experiencing in the moment, we can choose to respond differently.

On hearing the news about the new senior hire, there is obviously no way of immediately knowing what the truth is, so you draw conclusions and make assumptions using your memory and belief system as a filter, to assimilate a better idea of what is going on. You could choose a negative frame by sourcing information from the part of your brain that reinforces the idea that this is a bad change. You may ask yourself questions that lead to negative conclusions. Why have they brought someone in above me? Does that mean they don't value me? Do they want to get rid of me? Seeing the down side of the change won't make you feel good. Remember, at this stage you don't know what is true, as you haven't been told. Yet the stories we create in our head can feel very true, and we can become anxious because of them.

Someone who has previously had good experiences with managers, and who is confident in their own ability, may see the change as positive and have less fears.

The stories we tell ourselves (the frames we use) about the situations we encounter have a significant impact on how we react to them, what we experience and how we feel. Those feelings can lead us to behave in a positive or negative way and can lead to rumination, which is not good for us. When we understand that our frames are simply the stories we're telling ourselves, based on past experiences and fears, we can choose to start telling ourselves different stories, and therefore experience life more positively.

How to Choose Better Frames

1. Recognize your frames – the more you understand your responses and how they make you feel (mentally and physically), the more conscious you become of them,

and the more you can gain control of them when they are unhelpful.

2. Explore the situation – rather than jumping to conclusions about what something could mean, run through a more extensive list of possible meanings. Keep on asking yourself the question: "What else could it mean?"

3. Pay less attention to the people around you – often others can choose a frame that isn't helpful for your situation, based on their own experiences, beliefs and the meaning they choose to apply. Hold your own counsel, and be more discerning.

Leadership Myths

1. What we believe is true.
2. You can't change the way you view a situation.

Get Conscious

Are the frames you are choosing more positive or more negative? Think of a recent situation that made you feel unhappy. How did you assign meaning to that situation? Was it useful in dealing with the situation? The next time you deal with a situation where you don't have all the information, notice how you respond and look at all the positive meanings you could apply.

LESSON 18

Stop Trying to Be a Superhero

We put ourselves under tremendous pressure to be perfect. We want to be high-performing, infallible, strong ... whichever adjective you want to use, our expectations of ourselves can be incredibly high. On top of this, we worry about how others see us, pretty much all of the time.[72]

The society we live in puts immense pressure on us to be perfect too – from the amount of money we make, to the way we look, to the type of parent we are and so on. This sugar-coated projection means that we feel a sense of underperformance or even failure before we even get out of bed in the morning. So, we spend a lot of time internalizing our disappointment in ourselves.

Whether we are conscious of it or not, we all have standards for ourselves, and when we don't meet them, we become frustrated, anxious, guilty, angry or upset. Everyone is different, with different standards. One person may expect to always land a business deal with a hot prospect; someone else may expect to never make a mistake on a report, or may want to be the best parent. Yet we can and often do fall short of our own arbitrary expectations. Regardless of your own superhero standards, such criteria creates unnecessary pressure and makes everyday life that little bit harder to live.

Life coach Fiona Buckland says that "these feelings can lead to intense self-criticism and destroy the possibility of feeling fulfilled. We then feel isolated, misunderstood and like our lives are disasters. We won't compromise, we resent negotiation, we overwork and refuse to let go and delegate, as we don't trust that other people will get it right."[73]

Often the need for perfection stems from the pressure we were put under as children, or if we feel inferior to others. But perfection is simply a construct of our mind, and unless it is a force driving us forward, it is not helpful and can have a detrimental impact on our performance and wellbeing.

We should also consider the impact our perfection standards may have on others. Parents who set unrealistically high standards can often put their children under immense pressure, as their tolerance for mistakes, mishaps or imperfection is lower. This is a problem for the developing child, whose growth often comes from making mistakes – that's how most of us do our best learning, right?

Leaders who have the need to be perfect can create a barrier between themselves and their team, and can be seen as being able to attain unrealistic or intimidating standards. Initially, this may be inspirational, but over time it can create stress and lead to exhaustion in team members. It can also mean that people feel unable to be honest when things aren't 'perfect' or go wrong. Additionally, when a leader gains a reputation for being a consistently high performer, it can create pressure for them to constantly achieve standards that are hard maintain – and this can lead to stress and burnout.

Showing vulnerability and allowing ourselves to be imperfect is vital for both confidence and resilience.

According to Alain de Botton, founder of The School of Life, "We are very focused on the downsides of vulnerability yet when we may dare to explain with rare frankness that we are afraid and that we do many silly things, rather than appalling our companions, these revelations may serve to endure us to them." This is because when others see we are imperfect, it allows them to be imperfect too.[74]

How to Be Imperfect

1. Notice your superhuman standards – when you start to pay more attention to yourself and your inner monologue, you'll notice what you're chastising yourself about. Once you become more aware of these standards, you can decide whether they are helping or hindering you.
2. Stay present – when you stay present and in the moment, you give yourself less opportunity to ruminate about all the ways you're falling short. When you do notice yourself doing this, make a mental note of it and then bring yourself back to the present moment.
3. Set new standards – when you know what your superhero standards are, you can choose to change them. By deciding whether your standards are based on a sound and reasonable rationale, you can start to build new, more realistic standards for yourself.

Leadership Myths

1. Other people are coping better than you.
2. By seeming strong, you motivate the people around you.

Get Conscious

Where do you feel you're falling short in your life? Where do you think you let yourself or others down the most? What standards have you set for yourself that lead to this disappointment? Where have these standards come from? Are they fair or realistic? Think of one standard you could adapt so that it was more achievable. How did your parents or teachers view your performance and abilities? How is this affecting you now?

LESSON 19

We're a Nation of Imposters

Imposter syndrome is a psychological pattern where we doubt our accomplishments and have a fear of being exposed as a 'fraud'. Valerie Young, author of *The Secret Thoughts of Successful Women*,[75] describes it as "always waiting for the other shoe to drop. You feel as if you've flown under the radar or been lucky. If you dismiss your accomplishments and abilities, you're left with one conclusion: that you've fooled them."

It is very common for people to experience these feelings, although most of us are unlikely to speak up about them. We believe that people will judge us unfairly if we show a lack of confidence, or if they realize we can't do something. And they may well do so (depending on their view of the world). So, we internalize these feelings, which in turn causes a low level of anxiety that impacts our day-to-day life. As well as anxiety, impostor syndrome can lead to additional mental health issues, such as depression, as we try to live up to some image of success, fearing that we might be exposed as unworthy and incompetent.

Having humility and an awareness of our knowledge gaps, skills or abilities means we have a better understanding of how we can improve, and where to focus our efforts. It means we manage any inclination to become arrogant, a trait most people don't value.

However, when this awareness becomes negative, and we start to question our abilities, we may start to feel inadequate and lack in confidence, and this can hold us back. It can impact our career, our willingness to take on new challenges and even our relationships.

Some people achieve great success despite their imposter syndrome, but unfortunately there are also many who don't. 'Imposters' often seek external validation to make themselves feel better, but this constant seeking of approval from others can lead to disappointment when it is not received, or when not enough of it is received. The irony is, many people with imposter syndrome are the more competent and able people in the workforce. They have nothing to hide. Yet they're consumed by their own doubt.

Sometimes changes in circumstances can bring about imposter syndrome, even when people have never experienced it before, or when doubts in their abilities have not caused them problems. Losing a job and starting a new one, or ending a relationship, are some triggers for these insecure feelings and can lead to people losing confidence – even if it's not happened to them before.

Perfectionism and imposter syndrome are closely linked, and this often affects people who are doing a good job. These people are seen as valuable to the organization, yet their self-image does not reflect that value, as they have such high standards for themselves.

That's why the idea of growth mindset is useful to those who experience imposter syndrome. When we know that intelligence is malleable and that we continue to learn and develop, it helps us understand that we are on a journey, and that we are still learning. So, even if we do have gaps (which most of us do), it doesn't matter, as we're always learning how to fill them. Stanford lecturer Carol Dweck has developed the growth mindset concept over decades of research.[76] She has found that the most high-performing individuals tend to have a growth mindset, which means they are driven by the need to learn. They focus on mastering tasks and perceive failure to be a part of the learning process, so are less likely to experience inadequate feelings. However, people with a fixed mindset see intelligence as a fixed entity, and tend to be motivated by 'performance goals'. They are driven to prove their intelligence, blame themselves for failure, and experience anxiety and shame.

By recognizing that the internal voice telling us we are not good enough is not real, as it is a voice from our past or based on our own unrealistic expectations, we can become more compassionate with ourselves and more objective about our inner monologue.[77]

Although we may be high-performing and not even recognize it in ourselves, sometimes being good enough is all that we need to perform well and to succeed.[78] Donald Winnicott, a British paediatrician and psychoanalyst, came up with the concept of 'good enough parenting'.[79] This recognizes that it is unhelpful and unrealistic to demand perfection in parents, and when we do, it undermines the efforts of the vast majority of parents, who are in all practical respects 'good enough' to meet their children's needs. It also sets unrealistic standards for children too.[80]

If we adopt the same philosophy in our wider lives, the concept of being good enough removes much of the pressure we put ourselves under to be a model citizen, and means we are less likely to feel like a fraud. When we remove this stress, it helps our wellbeing.

Make Friends with Your Inner Imposter

1. Most people feel the same way – many of your problems stem from believing that others have better control over things, that they are saner and more intelligent, but in reality, most of us are thinking the same about each other. You need to realize that it's often just 'smoke and mirrors', as everyone it trying to project the best version of themselves.
2. Believe in 'good enough' – when you lower the benchmark for what 'good' looks like, you remove some of

the pressures of trying to be something you don't actually need to be.

3. Show yourself some compassion – letting yourself off the hook when it comes to knowing all of the answers, or being 'smart', can be very liberating. When you believe that you are still learning, along with everyone else, you can be kinder to yourself.

Leadership Myths

1. Everyone else is more 'together' than me.
2. The voices in my head are true – I'm a fraud.

Get Conscious

Do you ever question your ability or competence? What is it about yourself that you question? Is that a voice from your past repeating itself? Do you seek validation from those around you? When is that most prevalent? What are you good enough at? How could you apply the 'good enough' idea to other aspects of your life?

LESSON 20

How Well Are You?

Often, at work or in our personal lives, we forget about ourselves and our needs. We want to keep other people happy, do what's expected of us and achieve as much as we can. We put many of our own needs and desires to one side, to function effectively, to cope with demands and to take care of others' wants and needs. The problem is, when we spend our time meeting the needs of others, we can very often end up neglecting our own. In the short term this can work; in the long term, it can leave us feeling unfulfilled, ineffective and as though we're not progressing in the right direction. It can stop us from growing. And it can certainly affect our health.

Many of us aren't aware of what enhances our wellbeing, and also don't necessarily know when we're not feeling or performing at our best. We are so used to doing what we do, and feeling what we feel, that we just get on with it and don't expect anything else. Even when we know we should change things, we struggle to. We know we should leave the office on time, but we don't. We know we should do more exercise, but we don't. We know we should see the kids more, but we fail there too. We may achieve our daily task list, but if something has to be sacrificed, it's normally the aspects of our lives that are likely to enhance our own personal wellbeing.

Keeping our bodies nourished, getting enough sleep, having fun, spending time with loved ones, getting time for exercise, spending time on the hobbies we love, doing a job we love ... you name it. It's the things that can profoundly enhance our lives that suffer. What makes matter worse is that we often don't see what's missing, and the impact this absence is having.

This constant state of compromise and neglect of our own needs is no good for us or our wellbeing, or our growth as individuals. Many of us don't realize this until it's too late. That was certainly my experience, and it's why I reached burnout.

Work can push us to the max. Whether our employers expect it from us or not, we can spend a lot of our energy focusing on work. Unless we consciously manage ourselves better and keep a good balance, we end up our own worst enemy. And when managers see you working hard, they won't necessarily realize the sacrifices you're making. Some managers wouldn't care, but many wouldn't expect you to miss out on other parts of your life for work. They'd expect you to manage your time and energy better.

Hard work is great, passion is awesome, but not when it means that our own needs, our health and our relationships are compromised. This is where you need to take more control.

Yet many people miss medical appointments, sports days, birthdays, family holidays, time for fitness, time to see the kids and their partners, and time for themselves. Not just because the culture dictates it, but because they haven't thought about what to do instead.

Working parents struggle with this balance even more acutely than many others, according to Anna Meller, owner of Sustainable Working Ltd. Previously, the division of labour was clear; normally, men went to work, and women stayed at home to look after the children – easy. Men were 'separators', able to remove themselves from home in order to go to work, and that was their main focus, while women ran the home. Now parents are having to work together as 'integrators', which means men and women alike balancing the varying needs in their lives. It means we all need to be better at speaking up about our needs, not just in our relationships, but with our employers too.

How to Meet Your Needs

1. Where are you starting from? How well are you feeling now? Ask yourself these questions:
   - When I am at my happiest, what am I doing? (you may have a list of things)
   - When I have a great day at work, what has happened?
   - When I have a great day off work, what am I doing?
   - What are the relationships that nourish me the most?
   - How often do I spend time on those relationships?
   - To what extent do I feel I am growing as a person?
   - What are my five biggest stressors?
   - What habits are getting in the way of me being more effective?
   - Am I getting enough support, in my work and/or home life, to succeed?
   - On a scale of one to ten, how good is my wellbeing?

   These questions won't give you all of the answers. They will give you a greater understanding of how you're feeling and where you can make improvements.

2. What do you want instead? Visualizing how you would like to work, and what you would like your like to look like, can help you paint a picture of where you want to get to. What you want in your life. How you want to feel. Who you want to be spending more time with. What you want to be doing more and less of. Once you get that clear in your mind, you can take the next step ...

3. What one thing can you do differently today? What boundary can you set about the way you work that you will not compromise? What hobby or activity can you take up that will enhance your wellbeing and help you to reenergize? What are you no longer prepared to compromise on? What one thing would have the most

significant impact on your wellbeing? What are you going to do to change/make it happen?

Leadership Myths
1. We work in the way we do because it makes us happy.
2. People tend to know what enhances their wellbeing.

Get Conscious
Do you ever reflect on the way you are working? Do you feel you have a good balance, and if not, do you ever feel in balance? What habits have you slipped into that are not helping you? When you decide that you want to change something about your routine, how do you plan to make that change? How much do you suppress your deepest needs? Why do you do that?

LESSON 21

Moving to a More Mindful World

Mindfulness is an ancient art that keeps us focused on what we're doing. In the workplace, it has been linked to improving productivity and reducing sickness, so it's easy to see why more and more employers are investing in it. At an individual level, it can improve job satisfaction and work/life balance, reduce burnout and stress and positively affect our overall wellbeing.[81]

Mindfulness is a component of the wider art of meditation, not a form in itself. For millennia, mindfulness has been used as a tool to help the brain work more effectively so we can stay present and keep calm. We are largely automatic creatures, and the brain creates habits of thought and behaviour to function effectively by 'programming' itself based on past knowledge, experiences, beliefs and values. That means the 'data' that goes into our brains each day is creating our reality. Although we don't realize it, that data is skewed, and what we think and believe isn't true or accurate, so we overreact and ruminate. This creates negative feelings based on the 'stories' we've created in our minds, and not the reality. No one is immune to this – it's human nature.

Simon Michaels founded Mindful Work to give companies better access to mindfulness. His courses and apps boost wellbeing and productivity by helping people stay focused on the present moment experience, and to react and respond with more emotional intelligence. Simon says there is only so much we can perceive in the world around us based on the tiny three-degree cone that is our visual field. Everything beyond is made up of inexact visual information and a lot of memory. That means our reality, the one we live in every day, is largely made up of what is going on inside our brain and not outside. It gives us the capacity for amazing creativity and imagination, but it also means we manufacture much of what we believe to be true, especially as we tend to reinforce what we already believe. Therefore, if we doubt our abilities in some way, we will unconsciously seek information to support that view. In contrast, if we believe we are going to win the race, we will seek data and take action that will likely lead us to a more positive outcome.

The challenge is how to discern between what is true and what isn't, and manage the emotional responses to our thoughts. This is where mindfulness becomes helpful, not only by helping us pay better attention to what is going on around us, and our reaction to it, but also by helping us gain wisdom and better insights into who we are, so we can choose to make changes.

Although mindfulness programmes in the workplace tend to focus on reducing stress, mindfulness can also be used to improve overall wellbeing, compassion and productivity.[82]

Mindfulness keeps us focused on present-moment awareness, and by practising this intentionally, concentrative ability increases. This also helps generate calm and clarity. Meditation is the broad term for gaining insight into the nature of mind. It means working on three aspects of brain physiology:

- The prefrontal cortex – which allows us to make good decisions
- The parasympathetic nervous system (PNS) – which calms us
- The limbic system – which controls our emotions

MRI scans have shown that after an eight-week course of mindfulness practice, the brain's 'fight-or-flight' centre, the amygdala (part of the limbic system), appears to shrink – which is said to be a good thing. It also reprogrammes the neural pathways that lead us to think and behave in the way we do, changing the structure of the brain. In other words, our primal responses to stress seem to be superseded by more thoughtful ones.[83]

Mindfulness also improves self-control, so that resisting distractions becomes easier when we are less impulsive and can make better decisions. It has also been found to strengthen resilience, helping us to better face setbacks and challenges.[84]

Mindfulness is as effective for our brains as exercise is for our bodies. It's just harder to see it making a difference. It's becoming so mainstream now that it's being practised by organizations like Google and the House of Commons, and because it can be integrated into daily activities, it can take no extra time at all. With practice it can revolutionize the way that you feel.

How to Become More Mindful

1. Focus on your breathing – simply drawing attention to your breath, breathing in through your nose and out through your mouth a number of times, triggers your parasympathetic nervous system and slows down a racing mind. Repeating this throughout the day when you are feeling stuck, stressed or tired, or when you have an extreme emotion, can help you get back in control. This takes practice, as with any new skill, so keep on trying and you will get better at it. You can do this while you work.

2. Take time out – sit down with your feet on the floor and your back upright, and spend a few minutes breathing in and out with your eyes closed. All of your attention should be focused on your breath, and when your mind

drifts off, which it will, bring your attention back to your breath without judging the drift – it's normal. You can do what's called a 'body scan', slowly scanning up and down your body to notice, in the present moment, how you are feeling, and whether there is any tension in specific parts of your body. Direct your breathing to those parts.

3. Take a walk – focus on each step, on your legs moving, on feeling your feet in contact with the ground. Focus your attention on walking and your surroundings, and when you get distracted, bring your attention back to the present moment.

Leadership Myths

1. Meditation is for hippies.
2. I haven't got time to meditate.

Get Conscious

How easy do you find it to stop and just breathe? How much notice do you take of your surroundings? How easy do you find 'staying in the moment'? How could feeling more focused and/or calm improve your work? How often do you feel frustrated, agitated or overwhelmed? How do you feel when you focus on your breathing instead?

LESSON 22

Facing Very Human Challenges

On a daily basis, we face numerous challenges, both in the workplace and in our personal lives. We're talking about things like menopause, mental health and financial stress. These challenges are quite commonplace, yet many are still considered taboo.

Statistics show that in the UK, one in 10 people have some degree of dyslexia,[85] 10% of women consider quitting work due to menopause[86], and money is the biggest cause of stress,[87,88] with almost one in five people losing sleep because of it.[89]

Yet there's very little happening in the workplace to support people facing these challenges, and most leaders do not understand their impact unless it is something they themselves have to face. Sometimes, the consequences of these challenges, and the lack of understanding and compassion around them, can lead to people being perceived as ineffective or underperforming. Although wellbeing is primarily an individual's own responsibility, work is the leading causes of stress, so employers have a responsibility to help ease the burden. Leaders have an obligation to understand what people have to face and create a suitable environment that optimizes performance.

This chapter only scratches the surface of this subject, as there are numerous mental, physical and life challenges that employees deal with. The point is that unless we look below the surface of what is going on, we can often end up treating the symptoms, rather than helping to address the cause. If employees are fearful that raising their problems could put them at a disadvantage, they will be less likely to speak up about them. Leaders have a role to play in allowing people to 'be human'.

Menopause

Kate Usher, founder of second: phase, is a font of knowledge when it comes to the topic of menopause. She opened my eyes to the challenges women face in the workplace, describing menopause as something which 'completely devastated her life' and the reason she was driven to work in this field. According to Kate, 75% of women will suffer with some symptoms of menopause, and for 25% of these women, the symptoms are debilitating. The variance in age and duration, symptoms and severity is considerable. No two women experience menopause in the same way.

Although the average age of menopause in the UK is 51, women often start experiencing symptoms in their 40s, and these can continue well in to their 50s. And the social perception of menopause is that it's an older woman's condition, yet one in every 100 women experiences menopause before the age of 40. This doesn't include women who experience a medically induced menopause due to a hysterectomy or cancer treatment.

The list of symptoms is long. The 'superstars', according to Kate, are hot flushes, which can wake women anywhere from once to twelve time a night; mood swings, causing emotional outbursts ranging from rage to tears; weight gain; and irregular periods. The not-so-familiar yet all-too-common symptoms include anxiety, depression, loss of verbal recall and social confidence, memory loss, extremely heavy periods (commonly known as flooding), insomnia and intense exhaustion.

It's been found that 75% of women experience symptoms for an average of eight years, and many women hit menopause just when they are pushing for middle or senior management.

Hormone replacement therapy (HRT) is the only medication prescribed for menopause, yet there are associated health risks. There are a host of nonprescription options available, and women often have to go through a process of trial and error to find something that works for them. Talking therapies can also help.

There's no getting away from menopause. Every woman will have it at some point in her life, but according to Kate, there are many things that can be done to ease the experience.

For something so serious, affecting so many people, menopause is still barely recognized, let alone discussed in the workplace. It is no surprise, therefore, that the workplace response is patchy at best, and nonexistent in some cases.

At an organizational level, simple solutions can have a positive impact. Flexible schedules can help women who are struggling with symptoms, and having somewhere quiet to go can give them the space they need when their emotions become too much. USB desk fans are a cheap and effective solution for hot flushes, and for millions of women who have to wear uniforms, wearing trousers instead of tights, and natural fibres instead of man-made non-breathable fabrics, are a must. Every workplace should have proper sanitary facilities, and a place where women can change their clothes. Psychotherapy, counselling and coaching can be massively helpful, as they give women the opportunity to discuss their experience and identify possible solutions.

At a management level, there needs to be training to develop an understanding of the subject, enabling better conversations. Given that women have no control over menopause, it's not helpful when leaders become impatient.

This is the iceberg scenario – what you see is only a small fraction of what women are actually experiencing.

At an individual level, women need to know they have someone to speak to in the organization, and that they can request help if they need it. There is a real fear among women that admitting to menopause will negatively impact their reputation, and in the long term, their career prospects. Sadly, it is not unusual to hear of women leaving the workplace rather than discussing the impact of their symptoms.

Most women simply don't know what to expect when it comes to menopause, and they can often feel like they are 'going mad'. Very often someone else will notice that something is happening to a woman before she does, and with depression a very common side effect, it can be an extremely emotional time for a woman, signalling the end of her reproductive life.

As Kate says, there is nothing else that is covered by an organization's wellbeing budget that has such as impact on such a high percentage of the workforce for such a sustained period of time. The more support women receive during this time, the easier it is for them to deal with it – and to maintain their performance levels as well as possible during this time.

When leaders and peers understand what is going on, they can make sense of the changes they are seeing. According to Kate, when the individual emerges on the other side, they can be stronger and more focused than they were before. It's just a case of getting through the difficult part – potentially all eight years of it.

Dyslexia

Dyslexia is defined as a learning disability, yet many of us don't understand what dyslexia is or how to support those who have it. As a client of mine with dyslexia explained: "Expressing things verbally may be straightforward, but when it comes to writing things down, that's harder, and you may lose the impact of what you're trying to convey."

Often dyslexia is diagnosed at school, but this is not always the case, especially in individuals who learned coping strategies early on in life and don't present the tell-tale signs. This means that some people may not even be aware they are dyslexic. There are a variety of online symptom checkers, including one run by the Dyslexia Association, which can help you decide whether a full assessment is needed.[90]

According to Su Menzies-Runciman, owner of Ventures with Vision, a company that works with employers to improve culture, says once people are diagnosed with dyslexia, it can be a huge relief, as they understand why they have been feeling different and struggling so much with a whole host of challenges.

It's up to employers to create an environment where people are comfortable to say they have dyslexia, so that dyslexics aren't just seen as people who don't communicate properly. Su can get tongue-tied and forget the word she means to say, so it can be easy to wrongly assume the dyslexic person is slow to make decisions. Dyslexia can also lead to short-temperedness if people are struggling to be understood, and this can affect relationships both in and out of work.

Some ways in which leaders can help dyslexic individuals is by making presentations available electronically so they are not under pressure to take notes, or by providing laptops or electronic notebooks, as these are often easier to use than writing by hand. It's also important not to pressure such individuals into making presentations if they are not comfortable doing so, and to offer resilience training so that they can learn to manage stress and build their confidence. Giving them the space to take a deep breath and restart the sentence without feeling pressured can also lessen their anxiety.

When leaders hear the word 'dyslexic', they often assume the person is 'stupid' and mentally write them off. People with dyslexia are often very intelligent and have strong skills in areas such as design, problem solving, creativity and socially. Many successful leaders and business owners are dyslexic. Think about the strengths of the people on your team and how they can help each other. If someone is dyslexic and needs to write a report, just consider that they may need longer to do it. Allow more time for reviews and suggest using tools such as voice dictation.

Financial Stress

Although it's not necessary to spoon-feed people about how they should spend their money, employers can alleviate some of the stress people experience by providing better financial education and access to financial products, so that employees are fully informed and can make better decisions about their money. Gethin Nadin, author of *A World of Good* and Director of Employee Wellbeing at Benefex, is passionate about this subject. Gethin explained that whether it's an employer's duty or not, financial stress affects employees' productivity and can lead to distractions, supressed performance and the need to take time off. It is estimated that this stress costs UK businesses £120 billion a year.[91]

Financial education in the UK is the poorest in Europe, and although it has been incorporated into the education system, it's often dropped in favour of other 'priority' subjects. Yet managing money is an essential life skill that many of us don't have and around half of all people don't actually understand the basics of pensions and mortgages.

Surprisingly, as Gethin explained, financial stress often has nothing to do with debt, and high earners get financially stressed too.

When people get to grips with how to manage their finances and their financial patterns of behaviour, they can alleviate much of the stress they face. Through being a bit more planned, through recognizing our emotions around money and through a bit more understanding about how we can get the best from what we earn, it lessens stress. Yet we often avoid dealing with it; we know we have to, but it falls down the priority list. This is why Jo Thresher set up her company, Better with Money, to help people reduce the financial misery and confusion they were facing. Jo now works with employers to make the subject of money and how to manage it more interesting, and employees are changing their lives because of it.

Organizations have the opportunity to provide better information and recommend services and tools that can help employees get the right help and plan better. Opening up the conversation in the workplace removes the taboo and enables people to get in control, minimizing the impact of financial stress on their performance and wellbeing.

How to Support Human Challenges

1. Talk about it – and remove any taboo associated with these subjects. When people can speak up about what they are going through, without fear of judgment, they will share more. This not only alleviates stress for individuals, but also provides a greater understanding of what is going on, so that leaders can offer better support.
2. Provide education – create a designated area where employees and leaders can access good quality information about these topics, providing access to support services across a range of different subjects. Although

employee assistance programmes (EAP) can be useful, they are not a panacea for dealing with all of these issues. Find tailored and specialist support wherever possible.
3. Training – train leaders on these issues and improve their capability to have better quality conversations about them. Leaders also need to know where to sign-post employees to get more help.

Leadership Myths
1. People should leave their problems at home.
2. It's not up tp employers to support people with their personal problems.

Get Conscious
How comfortable do you feel talking to people about 'human challenges'? What leads to this discomfort? Do you jump to conclusions about why people aren't performing? Do you ever probe to find out what may really be going on for people? Do you know anything about the topics mentioned in this chapter? Do your fellow leaders? How could you open up the conversation about it? How could you be more open/supportive with your team?

LESSON 23

Know When to Quit

Andrew 'Bernie' Bernard from Innovative Enterprise works with young people while they are still in school to 'bring the future to life' for them. Having spent 17 years in the wrong job himself, he realized the importance of raising awareness among children of the careers available to them. With this goal in mind, Bernie is part of a National Careers Week group, providing support for educators to keep career education up to date.[92]

The educational system and the advice we receive about careers can pigeonhole us at a young age. We can end up following a career path without giving a huge amount of thought to why we are doing it, and whether it plays to our strengths and what we love to do. It can lead to us feeling dissatisfied in our jobs years down the line. By getting in front of children at an early stage and showing them what careers are likely to be available to them in the future, Bernie helps children make better choices.

If you are lucky enough to be in a job you love, then good for you. Those 'unicorn jobs' are few and far between. Statistics show that many people are dissatisfied in their career, because the role doesn't satisfy them, because the environment they're in doesn't suit them, or because they don't feel supported by their manager.[93]

There are a number of reasons why we stay in jobs that are not suitable for our mental health or our personal and professional growth. Some of us believe that giving up means we have failed. We paint a picture of what the job should have looked like, and when the reality falls short, again we blame ourselves. Some people simply don't have the confidence to leave, often because their self-confidence has been eroded working in a job or environment that isn't right for them. Others are in a money trap, dependent on their salary and fearful they won't secure the same income elsewhere. Some presume they will not find anything better, even if they did explore the job market.

Being dissatisfied at work can have a damaging impact on health. One study has revealed that people in the poorest quality jobs show a greater decline in mental health than those who are unemployed.[94] That means being out of work could be better for you than being gainfully employed.

There is growing body of evidence that shows how low job dissatisfaction can lead to mental and physiological problems such as burnout, low self-esteem, anxiety or even heart disease. It's clear that unless our needs are being met at work, we can suffer, even if we're not consciously aware of the damage being done.[95] Aside from the health effects, bad working conditions restrict our ability to show our true capabilities and reach our full potential.[96] There are numerous reasons for feeling dissatisfied at work, including mundane or repetitive work, lack of autonomy, not fitting in, not being listened to, being overworked or simply not be paid enough.

Understanding the long-term impact of staying in the wrong job or the wrong organization can help us prioritize what's important and take action.

How to Know Whether to Stay

1. Ask yourself when you were last happy – our lives are constantly evolving and even if you once enjoyed your job, you may not now. When you consider when you were last happy and why, it can draw your attention to what's missing and what you're compromising.
2. Consider how you are feeling – we often neglect to pay any attention to this. We go from day to day being

focused on the task ahead, and not on ourselves. When asked, we say we're 'fine'. But are we?

3. Is there anything you can change – sometimes it's the way you're framing the situation that needs to shift in order to improve the way you feel. If your expectations of what should be happening don't meet with reality, it can lead to constant disappointment. Often by shifting from optimism to realism we can better handle the environment around us.

Leadership Myths
1. I have to stay on my chosen career path.
2. I'll be fine if I just crack on.

Get Conscious
What makes you truly happy? When you were a child, what did you enjoy doing? Why did you enjoy doing those things? What do you enjoy now? Are there any similarities? Are you able to bring what you enjoy to your work? Are you playing to your strengths? What are you compromising for your job? A useful exercise to use is The Wheel of Life.[97]

CASE STUDY

The Power of Internal Champions
with Razeea Lemaignen

> ### Situation
> The British firm GlaxoSmithKline (GSK) is the world's sixth largest pharmaceutical company. Mindfulness courses at GSK form part of an Energy & Resilience programme and the company encourages employees to see mindfulness as a way to refresh their mind, focus better, be more productive and bounce back after frustrations.

Challenge

In 2014, Razeea Lemaignen, a project coordinator at GSK, started offering mindfulness taster sessions and sharing her own personal journey of how she used mindfulness to overcome panic attacks. Razeea believed that if people could learn to become more mindful, it would help them to be more compassionate towards themselves and others and would help people's wellbeing. With mindfulness having made such a positive difference to Razeea's confidence and resilience, she was keen to share the benefits with others in the organization.

Solution

Although it took a while to grow the programme, through Razeea's determination, popularity grew. In May 2015, Razeea was given a secondment as Health & Resilience

Specialist to offer sessions to employees globally. It was at this point that she did her mindfulness teacher training at Exeter University. The programme went from strength to strength and today, Razeea runs mindfulness sessions across 56 countries in three different time zones across Europe, the US and Asia Pacific – with up to 500 people dialling in to each session. People have the option of joining as an individual by 'live meeting' from their desk or from home or can join 'local champions' at sites that coordinate a room for employees to practise together.

Employees can also access recorded sessions at any time and because the sessions are run three times a day, people have the flexibility about when they dial in. The sessions are open to contractors too.

Outcome

Razeea is now training a network of internal champions around the company and the sessions have been translated into 15 languages. Ninety per cent of people have said that it has helped them manage pressure and stress at work with 99% saying it refreshes their mind, and 85% saying they can immediately apply the learnings. Razeea believes that sharing her own personal experiences has been helpful in breaking down barriers to people getting involved. It has also been important to educate people about what mindful meditation is, a mental exercise and technique that allows you to relate differently to your thoughts, emotions and sensory experiences. For many, they find it a deeply transformative experience.

CASE STUDY

Reframing Saved My Life
with Sean Ruane

Situation

A close member of my family passed away from cancer, and I bottled up my emotions and shut down. I didn't want my emotions to get in the way of doing well at university, and so I made a conscious decision to close down my emotions. The first few months were a 'success', and being a 'robot' meant that I was able to focus.

Problem

The problem was that, after a while, being robotic in nature and not facing up to my emotions began to alienate me from the people I was close to. I was depressed, and the people on the outside ended up suffering too. I totally isolated myself, and when I did go out, I learned how to smile to cover up how I was really feeling.

It felt like I was in a dark sea, and I felt lost. I didn't have any hope of things improving and had nothing to work towards. It felt as though there was no escape, and I tried to commit suicide. From my experience, I don't think people want to die, but they want the excruciating pain to end, and so ending their life is a practical solution. Thankfully, I realized that perhaps my life had a purpose, and when I came to the realization that my purpose was greater than my circumstances, it changed the game.

Solution

I started to realize that my emotions were being too eas-ily influenced by external circumstances that were often outside of my control. I was allowing events to happen 'to me', and I was dramatically affected by the actions of the people around me. Other people's perceptions of me really mattered, whether they were loved ones or even strangers, which meant whenever I didn't get the 'approval' I was looking for, I would internalize this feeling and it would eat me up.

I came to the realization that our conscious experience of reality is driven by the subconscious story we tell our-selves, and because my story wasn't healthy, I was being negatively affected. We are always seeking the approval of others and want our theories to be proved right, espe-cially our inner stories. I realized that if I was to become more resilient and avoid the negative feelings that had led me to suicidal thoughts, I had to change the story I was telling myself.

In my career, I had learned how to programme com-puters, and I liked the rationally driven way it worked. It created algorithms based on variables, and if you changed one variable, it would change the outcome. I realized that I could achieve similar results in how I thought and felt by changing my own 'variables'. So, if my internal variable was telling me that I was an 'imposter', then the external data that I received would interface with that variable and would produce that outcome – that I really was an imposter. Yet if I changed my internal variable to 'confident', then the out-comes would be very different. If I felt and thought that I was confident, I would start to feel more confident.

Having counselling really helped too. People are often sceptical of therapy, but the opportunity to speak about the way I felt in a safe environment really helped me to under-stand the emotions and deal with them.

Our stories come from our beliefs, and our beliefs are a repeated set of thoughts that solidify over time. By writing down affirmations and gratitude lists, and visualizing an 'ideal' state, slowly but surely you can begin to change your internal story - something that I now practise every single day, to this day.

Today

I am now a senior manager and help others dealing with mental health issues. My aim is to help a million people with mental ill health, as I know how debilitating it can be. From my own experience, I know that you can recover and come out stronger and more resilient than ever. By giving people hope – which we all need when we're going through tough times in our life – I know I can help.

RESILIENT

A Little Recap

Today, resilience is becoming increasingly important, as we need to be more agile and deal with ambiguity. As leaders, we need to minimize ambiguity where we can, but we must also support our people in developing positive mindsets and building confidence.

There are a number of steps that can be taken to improve resilience:

1. **Remove the stigma associated with mental health** by talking about it more and by better understanding it.
2. You must be able to '**put your own oxygen mask on**' before you can help other people effectively. Leaders who recognize the need to instil good working habits minimize the damage they are doing to themselves and others.
3. Understanding how to **take care of your brain health** is essential for greater mental clarity, productivity and wellbeing.
4. We have an instinctive need for certainty, yet when we **befriend ambiguity**, we build our resilience and ability to cope with change and circumstances outside our control.
5. We view situations in ways that are unhelpful to us. When we recognize that we can have greater control over the way we feel by **choosing better 'frames'**, we will minimize anxiety and improve wellbeing.
6. Stop trying to be a superhero, setting arbitrary standards for yourself to operate against. Recognizing that **being good enough** can be useful to improve the way we feel.

7. Stop comparing yourself to others. **Most of us are imposters** and suffer with self-doubt that can hold us back.
8. Recognizing **how well you are** can help you to identify where you need to make positive changes in your life. Once you know your starting point, you can begin to make positive changes to enhance your wellbeing.
9. Day-to-day pressures can be stressful and cloud our judgment. When we stop to **breathe and become mindful**, we give our brains the break they need to be productive.
10. We don't understand the myriad of challenges people face in their daily lives, such as menopause, dyslexia and financial stress. Through more compassion and **creating a safe space for conversation**, we can treat people more fairly and enable them to feel normal.
11. We must get better at recognizing when our job or working environment isn't doing us any good, and **know when to quit** for the sake of our long-term health.

AWAKE

We Are Less in Control
Than We Think

The Big Conscious Question:
What Is Going On, in and around Me?

The identity we assume as a leader influences our decision-making, thinking and behaviour. This means it is important for us to see who we really are and to know ourselves and our true identity. It means deepening our self-awareness through becoming more conscious. When we do this, we can take better care of our own needs and we can develop ourselves, personally, giving ourselves more choice to think and behave in a way that makes a positive difference and allows us to grow. It's what I refer to as Conscious Intelligence – the intelligence we need to wake up our true potential – and the potential of others.

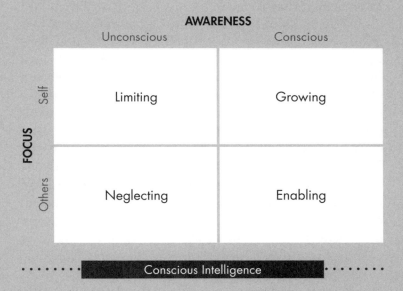

Our self-awareness and our ability to empathize and take care of the needs of others, has a significant impact on the way we feel and operate in our roles and how enabled others feel to operate in theirs. The more senior we become, the less we tend to inquire into ourselves (and often others), which means our Conscious Intelligence can suffer. Yet unless we understand ourselves as leaders and the impact we have on others, and unless we are able to take steps to get the best from ourselves and others, we are ineffective as leaders.

When we are conscious of our needs and our behaviours we grow and through being conscious of others and what they need, we enable them. When we are unconscious of ourselves we are limited. At best that means we make slow progress, at worst it means we're deteriorating and our mental health as well as our performance can suffer.

Although many people would consider themselves self-aware and in control of their own minds and their own performance, that's often not the case. This is not just because we don't know ourselves very well and we are oblivious to our own thinking patterns and behavioural traits, but also because much of what happens inside our minds remains hidden at a unconscious level, driven by a set of beliefs and values that have been created there. The unconscious mind automatically reacts to situations using stored data and behavioural responses, without the knowledge or control of the conscious mind. We are generally unaware of our behaviour, and most of the time we are unaware that we are acting unconsciously.[98]

Scientists have shown that most decisions, actions, emotions and behaviour depend on the 95% of brain activity that is beyond our conscious awareness. So, our life reflects our unconscious programming. This is because the job of the unconscious is to create reality out of its program, i.e. to prove the program is true. If you have negative programming in your unconscious, you will recreate those negative experiences in your life 95% of the time.[99]

Our unconscious is often not very helpful.

By getting to know ourselves and through becoming more conscious, we can take control of our lives and how effective and satisfied we feel.

And by learning more about ourselves, we learn about others too. Conscious intelligence leads to personal understanding and personal growth, and it also enables us to take better care of our wellbeing needs. Becoming more conscious of others, their needs and what brings out their best means we enable them too. Only through paying greater attention to the people around us, when they are at their best, and how our own behaviour as a leader is impacting their ability to do an effective job, can we properly support their wellbeing. We often don't recognize the impact of our thinking and behaviour on the people around us but through becoming more self aware and through learning more about how to optimise human potential, we can make a big difference to the working lives and the development of the people around us.

LESSON 24

Seek Self-knowledge

Given that most of us don't really know ourselves that well, isn't it fair to say you don't always know the impact you're having on the people around you? That means that if we want to perform at our best, and if we want to help others to do the same, we need to better understand how we 'show up', and how we use ourselves effectively – by developing greater self-knowledge – becoming more self-aware.

'Use of self' requires social sensitivity, an ability to accurately read the environment, and the capacity to react appropriately to situations.[100] It is much harder to do this when we don't know ourselves well.

The Johari window is a model developed by Joseph Luft and Harrington Ingham[101] to help people understand more about self-knowledge.

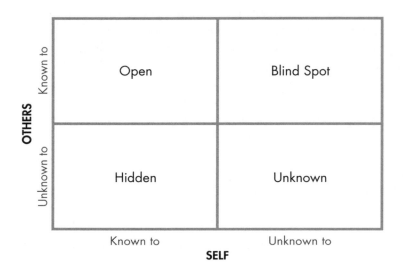

In this model, the 'open' area contains what we know about ourselves and that others know too. This could be things like our obvious strengths, hobbies, passions and viewpoints. In general, it contains things that we speak openly about.

But we also have a blind spot. This is what others see in us, but which we don't see in ourselves. Examples may include how we behave when we're under pressure or our hand movements when we're talking. These things can often be subconscious to us, but easily seen by others in our behaviour.

The hidden area contains what we know about ourselves but choose to hide from others. Biases, vulnerabilities and personal experiences that we are less comfortable talking about may sit in this area.

And lastly, there is an area that is totally unknown. We don't know this part of ourselves, and others don't know it either.

We are all a mix of all four of these areas. They represent our feelings, motivations, beliefs, experiences, views, attitudes, skills, intentions and behaviours, and are based on patterns of behaviour and thinking developed over our lifetime.

There are problems in not knowing enough about ourselves. Operating from a position of 'blindness', for instance, can lead to us unknowingly making decisions and behave in a way that negatively impacts ourselves and others. As a leader, that 'blind' type of behaviour can have damaging effects. The fact is, self-deception blinds us to the true cause of problems, and this can make matters worse, to the extent of undermining our leadership at every turn.[102]

When the 'unknown' areas are neglected, potential strengths are not explored or developed, and we can miss the opportunity to reach our true potential and achieve real fulfilment. Increasing our self-awareness not only allows us to unleash more of our potential, but also removes the mask that we wear to 'fit in'.

But how do we find out more about ourselves? It means critically assessing who we really are, getting more honest with ourselves about our traits and behaviours, and asking for more feedback. Unless we ask others for feedback and open up about our insecurities, it will be almost impossible to learn more about ourselves.

Becoming a better leader requires vulnerability, an open mind and a willingness to change, and feedback is a key ingredient in achieving that. Getting other people's views of ourselves allows us to appreciate who we are in a way that self-reflection alone simply does not achieve.[103] Leaders who ask for feedback have been proven to be some of the most effective.

And there are other benefits to exposing ourselves to the views of others – it leads to greater authentically. It allows us to let our guard down and be more authentic, which has a positive impact on those around us. It also improves our own psychological wellbeing because we can 'drop the act' and get closer to being who we really are.[104]

How to Build Self-knowledge

1. Ask for feedback – be open minded, keep defences down, and listen with curiosity about parts of yourself that you have yet to explore deeply. If other people see it in you, it's there, whether you see it or not. It's not just friends and family who can help; coaches and therapists help people with this for a living and can be a 'safe' starting point to discover more about who you really are.

2. Reveal more about yourself – by sharing more about yourself and who you are, you can build trust and understanding with others. This helps you remove the mask you may be hiding behind and reveal more

about yourself. It will open up conversations that help you understand yourself better.

3. Become more introspective – question yourself more and ask what the motives are behind your behaviour. When something doesn't go as planned, try to figure out the part you played in it. When the team is upset or seems frustrated, look at your own behaviour to see how you could have handled the situation better.

Leadership Myths

1. The more experienced you are, the more you know yourself.
2. Most people know themselves pretty well.

Get Conscious

Do you disclose information about yourself? If not, why not? How often do you reflect on your behaviour? When something doesn't work as planned, do you review the part you played and how you may have generated that result? Do you ever ask for feedback? If not, what scares you about it? Having been given feedback in the past, have you acted on it?

LESSON 25

Everyone Wears Masks

The idea of masks is an interesting one. Most of us are aware of the fact that we adapt our behaviour depending on where we are, and expose more or less of ourselves depending on the company we are in. But few are aware of how often it happens and why.

How many of your family and friends would recognize you at work? And do you feel able to express who you really are among the people you work with? The problem is that sometimes modifying our character to fit in with those around us, wearing a modified mask, can affect our ability to perform, as we're not acting as ourselves. And when we wear a mask for too long, it can be very demanding.

We normally choose our masks subconsciously, though, and have a chameleon-like ability to adapt based on the social cues we pick up on, hiding parts of who we are and bringing out others in order to avoid any negative judgements and often to convey a certain character, the one we think others would want to see.

Sometimes, we become so 'stuck' with the mask we wear at work that when we get home, we can't take it off. We continue to lead if we're a leader, we continue to support if we're a supporter, and we continue to make decisions if that is a key part of our role. This can be exhausting, and sometimes we want to ditch that mask and put on the ' invisible' mask.

Some days we can have an 'imposter syndrome' mask on and question our abilities; at other times we're having a good day and may turn up for work wearing a 'nailing it' mask. The masks that we wear are heavily influenced by our own emotions and beliefs – the views and opinions of others and the cultural norms that we become acclimatized to.

Just imagine the first time you were taken to meet your partner's parents for the first time. What mask do you think you wore in that situation? Probably not the 'unfiltered, say-whatever-you-think' mask.

Most of these mask decisions happen unknowingly. It is almost like we have a control centre inside that is constantly monitoring our surroundings in order to select the best mask for that moment. When we 'mask' ourselves, we are often concealing our real emotion and characteristics by portraying the most suitable emotions for that situation. We tend to do this to get the approval of those around us and to make a certain impact.

We all wear different masks for different reasons. Our childhood experiences have a huge bearing on the masks we choose to wear, as we learn very early in our lives what is an acceptable way of being and what leads to approval from others. Once again, this is subconscious. The upside of mask-wearing is that it helps us to better regulate how we come across in certain circumstances. The downside is that it takes away energy from our consciousness and, in the long run, wears out our energy.[105] Wearing masks at work can lead to us feeling insincere, dissatisfied, and emotionally and physically exhausted, and can even lead to health problems.[106]

Masks serve an important purpose, whether it's the 'functional mask' to show we're confident and able, the 'avoidance mask' that protects us from hurt and pain, the 'happy mask' that stops people from seeing how we're really feeling, and so on. Internally, masks make us feel safe; they protect our feelings. Externally, they can hide an awful lot of what is really going on inside us, and lead us to losing touch with who we really are.

So, there is a limit for mask wearing: too much of it can keep us from being our authentic self, and this can impact our long-term happiness. What if you were to drop the mask sometimes? Would it really be that bad?

How to Understand Your Masks

1. Look at the masks you wear – think about yourself in the various settings of your life. How do you 'show up'? What masks are you wearing? Why are you wearing them? Pay attention to the way you act and feel day to day. What emotions or feelings are you suppressing? Why can't you be yourself around certain people?
2. Express yourself – the key to mask removal is to be able to express your true self. Try this out. Begin to express your opinions and thoughts in a calm and gentle way.
3. Face what you're avoiding – we'll often be avoiding what we don't want to face as the pain or discomfort of confronting it is too much – this is why we wear the mask, as a cover-up act. This is where it is important to have someone to speak to, like a family member, friend, coach or therapist. Exploring what we are suppressing can be a journey for which we often need support.

Leadership Myths

1. I know when I'm suppressing my real self.
2. I have to modify myself to make others happy.

Get Conscious

How did you gain acceptance as a child? How did you know when you were doing something 'good'? How does that compare to how you seek acceptance now? What mask do you tend to wear the most? If you were to be your real self, who would that be? What would happen if you stopped wearing the masks? What would encourage you to lower your masks? What if people preferred the unmasked you?

LESSON 26

You Are Programmed to Repeat Patterns

Much of our behaviour is automated and based on patterns that have been hardwired into our neural programming over a lifetime. Patterns of behaviour can also be inherited, which means that we don't only inherit our hair and eye colour from our parents and grandparents, but also our attitudes and behaviours. Any activity can become a pattern or habit if repeated often enough, without us even knowing this is happening.

Making or breaking a habit requires neuroplastic changes in the brain. For example, someone with an addiction may desire something because their neuroplastic brain has become sensitized to the substance or experience and craves it. When an urge is satisfied, dopamine, a feel-good neurotransmitter, is released. The first time you do something, the dopamine reward happens after the event. Each time thereafter, dopamine gets released earlier and earlier, until just thinking about the event causes an anticipatory dopamine surge. The dopamine preceding the action motivates you to perform the behaviour in the future.[107] That's why we pick up our phones so much and eat too much chocolate. Well, speaking for myself.

It happens with behavioural and emotional patterns too. Once patterns of behaviour or emotions set in, they run permanently and unconsciously in the background, they become part of our programming. The more often we perform an action or behave a certain way, the more it gets physically wired into our brain. This is called 'neuroplasticity': how the brain changes its physical structure and function based on input from our experiences, behaviours, emotions and thoughts. This is why you always respond in the same way when your mum calls, or when your partner asks you to do 'that thing'. By recognizing that you are simply repeating a pattern of behaviour, you can choose to respond differently in the future, thus changing your responses to get better outcomes.

But changing behaviours can be quite tough. We know we want to quit smoking, cut down on sugar, go to bed earlier, meditate every day, stop getting angry and so on, but these things have become part of our neural programming, and to change them requires focused effort and attention. Although it can be difficult, it is very possible to change behaviours and habits.

Simply asking people to change tends to be ineffective. We've all experienced situations at work when there is an announcement about a change – we find that most people ignore it and carry on as before. They're not focused on making the change.

Our brain can only cope with focusing on so much at any one time, and becoming intentional and more conscious about a goal takes us a step closer to changing a habit or pattern of behaviour. When our brain knows it is going to be rewarded for our efforts, it focuses more attention on the goal. Breaking goals down into small steps, and monitoring the progress being made, helps us to maintain effort too. As we repeat these new actions, our brain reinforces new neural pathways as it would with any new experience,[108] hardwiring the new behaviour until it becomes automated. This is the process of learning, and age is not relevant. Neuroplasticity and learning can take time and effort but enable us to make valuable changes to our brains and not limit ourselves.[109]

Leadership Myths

1. People can't change.
2. If I just wait, things will change.

How to Change Your Behaviour

1. Decide on the habit or behaviour that you want to change – get clear about what you want to achieve instead of what is currently happening. In other words, what will a successful outcome look like?
2. Review what will stop you from making the change successfully – think about what will get in the way of you achieving the goal, and what you will do when those obstacles appear.
3. Set out a clear plan and practise – break the goal down into manageable stages and decide how you will reward yourself as you hit each stage. Think through a step-by-step plan for achieving your goal. Visualize the actions you will need to take to successfully achieve your goal. Then practise. Only through repeating the actions over and over again will you rewire what's in your brain. You may slip up – just keep going.

Get Conscious

What have you tried to change in the past? Did you have a clear plan in place? How often do you reward yourself when you achieve an aim or notice when you've made progress towards a plan? Where you have had success changing a habit in the past, what has led to your success? How could you use a similar approach to replicate the same success again?

LESSON 27

Do You Know Your Triggers?

You're having a great day, everything is going smoothly, and then someone says something and you feel annoyed, enraged even. It's out of the blue, and once you calm down, you're not sure why you reacted so badly. The comment was fairly innocuous, but you got emotional. You were triggered.

When we are triggered emotionally, it is an instinctual survival response. Our brains are programmed to look out for things that may hurt us. When analysing the situation, in a mostly unconscious process, the brain retrieves information from our past experiences, our values and our beliefs, and makes its best guess about whether what is happening is a threat.

Many of us are unaware of what triggers us, and that when we feel strong emotions in response to someone else's behaviour, it's often our brain's way of protecting us. Philosopher and author Alain de Botton explains that triggers happen very fast, and that there is no chance to observe the process: "Our minds are simply flooded with panic, we lose our bearings, the rational faculties shut down and we are lost, perhaps for days, in the caverns of the mind."[110]

Our brain gathers data, often making spurious connections with unconnected data from the past, and it jumps to conclusions about what is happening in front of us. We are often not reacting to what is happening at all, but drawing on information from a time when we were hurt in the past and applying the same rules and emotions to the new situation. So if we experience something in the present that seems to be similar, even in a small way, to an experience from our past, we draw comparisons and make the assumption that we could be facing a similar situation again. This inflates our reaction.

Take, for instance, your new boss. They call you into their office and ask you some questions about how the finances work. On the face of it, this seems like a reasonable request. They are new, they don't know how the finances work, and you do. However, your old boss used to give you a hard time over the smallest overspend and it became a real frustration for you. This new situation has no real relation to the old one, but your brain makes the connections, focuses on what feels similar and triggers your threat response as it fears a conflict coming. This is irrational. Your new boss is a completely different person than the one you had before. They are simply asking you some questions. You just need to give them some simple answers. This new relationship could be a whole lot easier than the last one, yet your brain has taken a short cut to an answer, and is telling you to defend yourself. You become defensive unnecessarily and it leads to an awkward conversation.

This is why relationships can often become difficult, purely through misunderstandings, perceptions and individual beliefs driving the wrong reactions. When we have had time to calm down, we often regret our initial reaction. Yet when we understand that many of our reactions are based on a default setting, we can be more forgiving of ourselves. That said, it's important that we don't just continue to overreact when faced with trigger situations.

In his book *The Chimp Paradox*, Professor Steve Peters refers to the 'Chimp', a representation of our limbic system, as an independent emotional thinking machine that works with feelings and impressions, and acts without our permission.[111]

In contrast, he suggests that another part of our brain, the 'Human', in our frontal lobe, allows us to think logically, and uses facts and truths to make a decision.

Either the Chimp or the Human can take control in any given situation, but when the Chimp takes control, he tries to protect us. In stressful situations, it is normally the chimp who reacts first, which leads to an over-emotional and often unhelpful response.

When we start to recognize our triggers and what leads to them, we become more conscious of our reactions. It allows us to slow down our reactions and to 'push pause' when someone says or does something, so that we can let our 'human' take control, minimizing the opportunity for our 'chimp' to go wild. Once we can take greater control of our triggers, we can improve relationships, our credibility as leaders and our mental health.

How to Get in Control of Triggers

1. Notice what triggers you – in order to take control of your triggers, you need to understand the situations in which you have a heightened emotional response.
2. Become suspicious – rather than give in to your feelings and emotions, when you are feeling annoyed, angry, anxious or aggrieved, question why this is. Is it based on what is happening now or could it be connected to what has happened in the past? Or are you just scared and your brain, your chimp, is trying to protect you?
3. Learn to read your physical reaction – very often you can sense that you are having a heightened reaction from the way your body responds. The sooner you notice what is happening, the quicker the human can take control. Watch out for increased rate of breathing, restriction in your throat, increased blood flow, tension in your muscles and constriction in your gut.

Leadership Myths

1. There is nothing I can do to control my emotions.
2. When I feel annoyed, it's based on what has happened in the moment.

Get Conscious

Do you notice when you trigger other people? Why may they be responding in that way? When someone else has a strong emotional reaction to you, do you question your own judgment? What gets you really upset? Have you experienced other similar situations in your past that may be exacerbating your reaction?

LESSON 28

Everyone Is Biased

There is no point avoiding it – we are all biased to some extent.

Some of us may have explicit biases that we are aware of as they happen at a conscious level, i.e. we dislike a certain group of people and are aware of it. Our implicit biases are built based on stereotypes that we have formed from our life experiences, but we are less aware of these. They form automatically without our awareness, so they can be difficult for us to notice, although others may notice them through what we say and the way we behave. The problem with implicit bias is that holding negative stereotypes means that we can treat people differently, even without us realizing it.[112]

Implicit bias can apply to individuals as well as groups or organizations, and the way they act as a whole. An example of this is a male-dominated working environment where women face larger barriers to success than men, even though they have the same talent, qualifications and ambition. In this situation, women themselves can add to the bias, as they may be influenced by the culture or experiences they have had.

Our biases can be against any social group. Age, gender, physical abilities, religion, sexual orientation, weight and many other characteristics are all subject to bias.[113]

Our brain tends to search for and focus on information that supports what we already believe, ignoring facts that go against our beliefs, despite their relevance. This is called confirmation bias, and we will consciously or unconsciously seek information and data that supports our views. Unless we tackle our biases on a conscious level, we will continue to reinforce them based on what we experience around us.

We also like to attribute reasons or motivations to the actions of others without concrete evidence. This is called attribution bias. It might inflate people, giving them a 'halo effect',[114] if we are very impressed by them. Or it can go against them, as we 'build a case' for why they are inferior or lacking in some way.

Our biases enable us to make quicker decisions, but they are often inaccurate, and can have a negative impact on our decisions when we are recruiting, career planning, viewing performance and interacting with others, either favourably or unfavourably. It can also lead to us building a skewed knowledge of a certain area, as we are only concerned with finding information that strengthens our argument.[115]

Even when it comes to the way that people think, by believing in neurodiversity, the concept that humans don't come in a one-size-fits-all neurologically 'normal' package, we stop trying to seek out people who seem 'right' to us. Instead, we recognize that all variations of human neurological function need to be respected.[116]

Although biases are deep-seated, they can be challenged and even changed.[117] We have to learn to become aware of what they are and be willing to acknowledge them, so that we can consciously override them.

How to Tackle Your Biases

1. Recognize that you are biased – question yourself more about where unconscious bias may push you towards a decision or action.
2. Slow down your decision-making – when it comes to others, repeatedly question yourself as to whether you're looking at the facts. Recognize this in other team members too, and talk openly about how bias could be impacting decisions, so you can tackle it.

3. Expose yourself to different types of people – and be curious about their backgrounds, their beliefs, the way they live, their interests. Through challenging your stereotypes, you will see more similarities between others and yourself, and this can break down some of the potential barriers.[118]

Leadership Myths

1. I am not biased.
2. I treat everyone the same.

Get Conscious

What are your biases? What type of people do you tend to avoid? Do you judge and categorize people based on their accent, what they wear, where they shop? What from your past has led to your making these categorizations? What data are you using to confirm your views? It is rational and reasonable? What is the potential impact on your team of the biases that you hold? How might they view you, based on some of the comments that you make?

LESSON 29

You Are Always Communicating

'Communication' is a term that is bandied around in leadership all the time. We talk about the importance of communicating with people, the need for engagement, that people need more communication during times of change, and how being open, honest and transparent leads to less ambiguity and improved morale for employees.

Most leaders understand the benefits of communication, both within their own peer groups and when dealing with their team members. Yet we are often not very good at it.

To understand this better, we need to understand what exactly we mean by 'communication'. Very often leaders see it is as broadcasting information to people. That, however, is only one part of the communication mix. Communication is about imparting and exchanging information, and so it's as important for all parties involved in the communication to have a voice.[119]

What else matters when it comes to communication? Well, it's the fact that even when we're not communicating, we are, in fact, communicating. Very often leaders think that saying nothing is better, as information unsettles people, especially during times of change. The reality is that when people are expecting to hear something and they hear nothing, they fill in the gaps. As I've mentioned earlier in the book, we don't tend to like ambiguity, and we will decipher what is happening, whether we are told or not. This can be catastrophic at worst and a distraction at best. Both affect performance. Sometimes this ambiguity affects mental wellbeing.

What can be more damaging, however, is when one party hears the information, but others don't. This can lead to confusion, uncertainty and false beliefs, and is a mistake that leaders often make unintentionally when they impart news to someone or a group, and don't plan well to share it more widely. A positive intent – to be open and to share – can turn sour if not enacted properly.

With today's shifting dynamics in the workplace, employees expect to hear more of both good and bad news. We are all adults, after all, and molly-coddling employees by protecting them from the truth is often unnecessary. Over 90% of employees say they would rather hear bad news than be kept in the dark, and some people even decide to leave organizations if they don't feel informed enough.[120]

The more people know, the more they feel enabled to make decisions and take control of the situations that may impact them. Very often, when organizations become more open in their approach, employees are motivated to take ownership for the changes required and take proactive actions to fix things. Grown-up communication leads to grown-up levels of responsibility.

The problem is that many leaders grew up in a more traditional or paternalistic environment, where the leaders knew what was happening and the employees didn't – or at least knew only what they needed to. In a task-driven environment, this parent-child dynamic may have been effective, but in the modern workplace, it's not.

Yet often for leaders to get more comfortable with open, two-way communication, they have to change. They have to challenge themselves to behave in a way that they are perhaps not comfortable with. Which means understanding what's getting in the way of you sharing and working with the team to discuss things more.

There are certain things that leaders may need to be more discreet about, where decisions are being made around structure or financial arrangements, but the sooner you get information to employees, treating them like adults and opening up the conversation, the easier the change will tend to be to manage.

How to Improve Your Communication Approach

1. Review what you do and don't tell people – critically assess whether holding information back is of any real benefit. Open up more, and see how this is received. It may take some time to get used to, but over time it will lead to a more open culture.

2. Ask the team for ideas – very often employees will have ideas on how to create a more open culture – they'll see the downside of the current culture. Asking them can uncover some areas for improvement. And then commit to making changes based on their recommendations.

3. Ask more questions – rather than staying on permanent transmit mode, open up the conversation. Ask people what they think, share issues that you are trying to resolve and ask for their input. This isn't about formal consultation. This is about being more grown up and honest in your approach without 'putting people at risk'.

Leadership Myths

1. People only need to hear what's happening when a final decision has been made.
2. Saying nothing is better than giving bad news.

Get Conscious

Do you regularly communicate what is going on to the team? If you're not clear yourself, do you try to gain clarity so you can update them? Do you hold information back, as culturally it is the done thing? How do you feel when you don't know what is going on? What is the impact when you are kept out of important decisions that could affect your future? Do you keep people updated as things develop or wait until you have a final answer? Why is this?

LESSON 30

Get Out of the Way and Listen

We often talk about coaching when it comes to leadership, but in order to coach, we must learn how to listen. This can be much harder than it seems, especially for leaders who are constantly having to solve problems, make decisions, make judgments and quickly assimilate information. In a leader's bid to help their people, they often hold centre stage, not realizing that they are dominating the conversation. The consequences are therefore often unintentional.

First, leaders can end up with the false assumption that they are the only ones interested or the only one to put forward ideas. Leaders who come up with a lot of ideas, and answers can end up suppressing the ideas of others. Others learn to stay quiet, with few opportunities to express their thoughts.

Second, when a leader is talking, they are not listening or reflecting. This can lead to all sorts of problems with creativity, innovation and new thinking. Diversity of thought is crucial to coming up with great ideas and when one or a few people dominate conversations, it can be harder to hear the voice of the wider group. Although less diverse thinking groups are typically more confident in their performance, the reality is that with more diverse thinking comes greater success.[121]

Issues go unnoticed unless leaders stop to listen. Perhaps it's because someone doesn't feel comfortable bringing something up or doesn't have the 'space' to. Regardless, a leader who is caught up in their own world and their own ideas and problems, and who is too busy hearing themselves, misses the opportunity to listen to people raising important issues.

Very often, people who talk a lot or who dominate the conversation won't be aware of the impact they are having. Counterintuitively, many will believe they are doing the right thing by taking a lead in the discussions, and see themselves as a better leader because of it.

Leaders who want others to take ownership, to think for themselves, to use their initiative, to be able to critically assess problems and to work out solutions, need to provide space for employees to do so. And this means listening. Enabling the group to work more collaboratively together leads to greater innovation, but there are many other benefits, including improved efficiency, improved operational performance, and higher levels of work-winning and client confidence.[122]

When leaders feel they are carrying the burden for the team's success on their shoulders, they need to ask themselves why this is happening. Often, it's their perception based on the way they have behaved to date, and therefore the responses they have been getting. Leaders who are the idea generators, and who make the decisions, can often feel overwhelmed by their workload and what they are facing. Some become frustrated with their teams, believing that they aren't 'stepping up' to help. This can lead to a self-fulfilling prophecy, which means team members become less likely to contribute.

The leaders who recognize the strength of group contribution can enable amazing results through watching, listening and drawing others in. Their voice facilitates the discussion but doesn't need to dominate it. Research shows that more extroverted leaders can feel threatened by proactive suggestions from employees, whereas introverted leaders are more inclined to listen closely to the ideas of team members and adjust. When a leader who listens understands that some team members may be less forthcoming with their ideas, due to their own characteristics, they will elicit feedback from everyone in the room and make sure people who are less likely to share their ideas in a group setting can share their thoughts in one-on-one conversations.[123] By listening to team members, you tend to also get better buy-in once a decision has been made.

How to Become a Better Listener

1. In meetings – listen and get others involved. Allow others to play a part in the meeting and share the agenda so you don't have to hold the floor throughout the meeting and listen to what people have to say. The more you do this, the more people will get used to it, and the more of a habit it will be for you.
2. Get curious – ask for people's ideas and thoughts inside and outside of meetings, and listen with interest without the need to give your viewpoint, ideas or a quick response. Give people time to cultivate ideas and come back with suggestions at a later date. Not everyone will have their ideas in the moment.
3. Say yes – and act on what you've heard, as this will have a significant impact, especially where people are used to 'not being heard'. When you go with ideas that others put forward, without tampering with them too much, it's motivational. The more you do this, the more people will want to contribute, and the more ownership they will take.

Leadership Myths

1. Leaders should be leading the conversation.
2. When a leader comes up with solutions, it encourages others to do the same.

Get Conscious

Do you talk too much? Does your team take ownership for ideas or solutions outside of their comfort zone? If not, what is it about your behaviour that may be affecting them? When you sit and listen, what happens? Do you want to jump in? What are you worried about if you let others take the floor? Do you believe that by talking a lot and having a lot of things to say, you are a better leader? Do you give people the space to think/time for reflection?

LESSON 31

Never Normalize Bad Behaviour

Organizations can often be riddled with bad behaviour, which can take many forms. Whether it's people turning a blind eye to the salesperson who earns a lot of money but isn't very nice to people, or the individual who is late for meetings yet has never been challenged about it, bad behaviour can cause stress and chaos for the rest of the team.

These people may not be aware of their bad behaviour and are unlikely to be bad people. The salesperson may not be aware that they offend people, the tardy employee who turns up late may not see themselves adding any value to team meetings.

We often see behaviour around us that isn't helpful. We're all human, and we all have bad days. The issues occur when the problem persists or when it is left unresolved. We should all take responsibility for our own behaviour and our impact on others, and when we see that an employee's behaviour is starting to affect their performance, it is time for this behaviour to be dealt with. Take the individual who is always missing deadlines. Their manager knows they do it; they know the impact it's having on the wider team and that others are having to pick up more work as a consequence, which is affecting their stress levels. The manager is struggling to have a conversation with the individual, as they don't know how to broach the subject and are worried that the individual is going to react badly. At the same time, the rest of the team is getting increasingly frustrated that the manager isn't tackling the problem, and this manager is starting to lose credibility.

When one person behaves badly and it's left unchecked, regardless of the reason, it has a ripple effect across the team and the organization. It leads to frustration, resentment, increased anxiety and suppressed performance.

We also avoid dealing with these situations when the person who is behaving badly is a high performer. We place their performance ahead of the greater good. Yet although on the face of it they are doing a good job, under the surface they are causing irreparable damage to other people's performance and wellbeing.

How to Deal with Bad Behaviour

1. Be upfront – have a conversation with the individual. The aim of the conversation should be to raise their awareness, the impact of their behaviour and what you expect to see instead. This isn't about blaming, punishing or victimizing. It's about stating the facts, having a grown-up conversation and asking the person for their input on the situation.
2. Hear their viewpoint – the individual may have personal issues or may genuinely have no idea of the impact they are having. See this as awareness-building. You need them to see the impact of their behaviour to give them a chance to self-correct.
3. Remember why you are dealing with the behaviour – it can be easy to give in when talking to someone about behavioural change, especially when they become defensive or reject your claims. Remember you are there to protect the wider interests of the team or organization and to make sure that everyone understands the standards expected.

Leadership Myths

1. You can overlook bad behaviour for high performers.
2. People know when they are behaving badly.

Get Conscious

Do you turn a blind eye to any bad behaviour? Why are you doing this? Are you taking responsibility for the wellbeing of your team, or are they being impacted by the behaviour of others? Who else should be taking responsibility for dealing with bad behaviour that you could speak to/agree a way forward with? Is any of your own behaviour bad? Are people struggling to tell you? How would you react if someone told you that you were negatively affecting people around you?

LESSON 32

Don't Believe Your Own Hype

Sometimes we get caught up in our own world and find it difficult to see what is happening in the worlds of others. It may be temporary because we have to deal with a specific situation that requires us to focus, and this is less of a problem for us as a leader. However, if we become consumed by what we are having to deal with or by our own needs for a longer period, then we may be having a negative impact on those around us.

People usually rise to power when they have qualities like kindness, good listening skills, concern for the greater good, enthusiasm, focus, high empathy and humility. Unfortunately, when people achieve these positions of power, these qualities are often forgotten, and self-entitlement, indifference to the plight of others, negative interruptions in conversation and a lack of basic politeness take over.[124]

Holding onto humility as you rise up the ranks is essential if you want to lead well, and you want to positively influence people. When we start to view our needs as more important and forget to think about the needs of others, we become less open-minded and more judgmental, which can inhibit our ability to learn and take on new ideas. All of these traits undermine our ability to be good leaders and can lead to greater team conflict.

The most common causes of interpersonal issues and conflict in organizations are concerned with people's view of their own sense of identity, status, importance and position. We tend to feel under attack (rightly or wrongly) when something occurs – if we have made a mistake, for example, or we perceive that someone is trying to gain a position of power over us that we see as unwarranted. At this point, many of us engage in what is called ego defence, which is the process of acting to protect our self-worth, our identity, our standing or our authority in the organization. This is when humility goes out the window.

There are two core elements to humility: low self-focus and high other-focus. Low self-focus means a lack of self-aggrandising, self-promoting and competitive behaviours, and being open-minded and wanting to learn. High other-focus requires a greater respect and acceptance of the values, beliefs, ideas, knowledge and experience of others, and striving to understand and be of service to others as well as ourselves. It also requires us to be honest.

Being humble is about having a lack of preoccupation with ourselves and our status, position, rank, authority and identity. It also means admitting and acknowledging mistakes and looking for the good in others. When people start to believe that they are responsible and accountable for their own behaviour, they are much more likely to engage and be motivated to learn to be humble. The starting point is to understand and acknowledge that people can learn, develop and change.[125]

How to Develop Greater Humility

1. Use inclusive language – like 'we', 'us', 'our', 'all', 'together', rather than 'I', 'they', 'them', 'my own'. This helps to reduce or break down barriers and hierarchies and emphasizes connection.
2. Recognize that your characteristics and traits are fluid – you can learn, develop and change. You are responsible and accountable for your own behaviour and can adapt your behaviour to place others' concerns above your own.
3. Think with more humility – think about how someone with humility would react in different situations.

What would they think, what would they do and what would they say? How does this differ from your behaviour?

Leadership Myths
1. Leaders need big egos to be successful.
2. I am who I am and can't change now.

Get Conscious
How do you feel if someone challenges your thinking? When you become defensive, are you listening to the other person's perspective and gathering the facts? How much time do you spend thinking about yourself at work in contrast to thinking about your team? How easy do you find it to credit others for their efforts? How often to you refer to your own successes and achievements in comparison to pointing out and celebrating those of others?

LESSON 33

Emotions Fuel Performance

One of the biggest taboos in the workplace and a subject we tend to avoid is that of emotions. Emotions are such a fundamental part of who we are, it's peculiar how they ever became taboo at work. When we think about commercialism, productivity and delivery, we probably don't think about emotions. Yet without the fuel that emotions provide, it's arguable that we wouldn't achieve any of these things.

We often suppress our emotions, despite the fact that they drive so much of what we do, say and feel. We've associated too much emotion with being a negative trait in a work setting (or even outside of it), and so we control ourselves in order to come across as calm, rational and balanced. This can be a good thing, because emotional intelligence requires the ability to regulate emotional responses. Yet there is a downside to suppressing our emotions. When we are unable to express how we really feel, negative emotions are strengthened, weakening our ability to think clearly, impairing our working memory and affecting our motivation and the effort needed to achieve goals. This causes us stress.[126]

Research shows that emotions lead to group cohesion and the ability to coordinate and achieve shared goals. That's because emotions are contagious, and we can be easily affected by the emotions of others. Heightened emotions like enthusiasm, hostility and anger tend to be 'caught' more easily than low-intensity emotions such as depression or sluggishness. This is probably why organizations are increasingly trying to find ways to keep employees 'happy'.[127] In contrast, holding on to negative emotions can lead to episodes of 'flooding out', where we spontaneously combust in an uncontrolled and unhelpful way.

Phil Wilcox, founder of Emotion at Work, explained that when we "relabel emotions", move away from positive and negative tags, and stop "judging people when they are emotional", we start to see emotions as a "normal part of the human experience. This enables people to express a full range of emotions without the need to constantly curate their character." Often, we react badly to others' emotions, as we don't understand where they are coming from. When we see emotions as a normal part of relationships and conversations, we judge them less, accept them more, and open up more dialogue about why we are feeling the way we are. It is less about suppression and more about understanding.

This requires us to be vulnerable and let our guard down. It is a huge relief when we learn to let go and allow ourselves to show who we really are and be 'emotional'. Brené Brown, a leading light on the power of vulnerability, suggests that "if we want true authenticity and power at work, we need to be willing to feel and acknowledge our emotions". And Google agrees.[128] Through extensive research, they have found that team effectiveness comes down to two things: 'conversational turn-taking', where everyone on the team gets time to speak, and 'social sensitivity', meaning the team is skilled at intuiting how others feel based on their tone of voice, their expressions and other nonverbal cues. That means understanding them emotionally and allowing people to express themselves emotionally.

However, expressing emotions without any consideration for how it may be received can lead to problems.[129] It can either be 'destructive', where we end up in conflict by retaliating or hurting another person, or it can be 'constructive', where we are able to express ourselves while at the same time being cooperative. We have to consider our own personal interests versus those of others if we want to generate good relationships with those around us. This is something that emotions expert Paul Ekman talks a lot about.[130]

In his book *Emotions Revealed*, Ekman explains that by learning the triggers for each emotion, the ones we share with others and those that are uniquely our own, we may be able to lessen their impact. One way of becoming more aware of our emotions is to watch what's happening in our bodies. This is because each emotion generates a unique pattern of sensations in our body, and by consciously recognizing those sensations, we may become aware early enough in our emotional response that we have a chance to either embrace or interfere with that emotion. Recognize the physical reaction early enough, and you can control the emotional reaction better.

Jeremy Dean from riders&elephants works with organizations to discover how people feel, using a tool called the Emotional Culture Deck. Having spent years working with organizations to help them define their values, he recognized that the starting point was actually identifying what the culture needed to feel like. And that required employees to talk about emotions. Jeremy noticed that leaders often fail to acknowledge people's emotions even though the emotional culture of an organization has a significant impact on employee satisfaction, burnout and teamwork, as well as influencing hard measures for issues such as financial performance and absenteeism. And because leaders often don't talk about emotions, because emotions are considered difficult or soft, they fail to display the empathy and openness that enable people to function better. Jeremy sees that teams expressing how they really feel leads to relief and liberation, because people can finally talk about the things they have going on inside. It helps people to relate and connect with each other in a way no other conversation can achieve. It builds trust and understanding, which ultimately help teams to perform better together.

How to Get More Emotional

1. Open up the conversation – give people time and space to express their views, their ideas and their feelings. Allow people to talk about why they feel good and why they don't.
2. Notice how others feel – get comfortable asking people about what is going on when they are emotional – get them talking. Don't brush signs of emotion under the carpet; instead, get emotions out in the open.
3. Ask people how they want to feel – have open discussions with the team about how they want to feel at work. Talk about what needs to happen in order for them to feel what they want to feel and make a plan to change the environment.

Leadership Myths

1. Suppressing emotions makes us feel better.
2. We have little control over our emotions.

Get Conscious

How comfortable are you with your own emotions? When someone wants to talk about their feelings, how do you react? When you see someone else appearing emotional, how likely are you to explore what's going on for them? Do you create a safe environment for people to be able to express themselves properly?

CASE STUDY

Taking Better Care
with The Insolvency Service

Situation

Nine civil servants from various government departments got together through the Civil Service Local Junior Leadership Academy in 2017. 'Team Chaffinch', as they referred to themselves, wanted to work on improving wellbeing; having made small changes at a team level, they saw an opportunity to provide something for the entire organization.

Challenge

Wellbeing is high on the agenda for their senior leaders, as part of the vision to 'create a brilliant Civil Service'. After carrying out some research, Team Chaffinch spotted an opportunity to help people take better care of their own wellbeing. They wanted to create something that could be tailored to people's individuals needs, and saw wellbeing as starting with good conversations with your line manager. They believed people's wellbeing would be bolstered if they were able to speak more openly about how they were feeling, their career expectations and learning opportunities, and by understanding what was going well and what needed to improve.

By encouraging more open dialogue, they wanted to raise awareness of what would lead to greater wellbeing, and promote better conversations and understanding.

Solution

It led to the design of the *A-Z to Better Wellbeing Toolkit* – enabling people to take small actions to improve their wellbeing every day. This curated kit brought together the latest wellbeing resources, best practice, stories and wellbeing journeys from colleagues around the Civil Service.

The toolkit, accessed from work or home, includes:

- 26 wellbeing topics (from A-Z)
- Wellbeing activities to do as individuals and teams
- Over 70 wellbeing ideas and suggestions
- Links to further learning, including Civil Service learning courses, Ted Talks and printable guides
- Top tips from around the organization

The team understood that one of the biggest barriers to focusing on our own wellbeing is time. This is why they featured many activities that could be done in under 15 minutes.

The activities included self-reflection, goal setting, team building, dealing with musculoskeletal problems, how to eat well and time management. The toolkit also covered how to deal with stress, giving access to useful helplines such as The Charity for Civil Servants, and advice on how to detox from social media and get better sleep. Volunteering and fundraising for a cause were also featured.

Through the creation of a growing Twitter community, they have kept people connected, with colleagues sharing their wellbeing success stories and giving each other support.

Outcome

The toolkit has been attracting some great feedback from around the Civil Service, and won Team Chaffinch a 2018 Civil Service Award in the Health and Wellbeing Category.

They were also one of the 26 winners in The Charity for Civil Servants Community Awards 2018.

The team have continued to promote wellbeing, sharing blogs that receive up to 50,000 views at a time. It shows that people are engaged, and the team is currently promoting the toolkit with a second wave of publicity, including various Civil Service blogs and Twitter posts.

It is too early to assess the overall impact of the toolkit, but the initial results are promising. The next goal is to take the toolkit on the road, and start hosting discovery sessions where the team can interact with the audience, and people can get involved with practical activities around wellbeing.

CASE STUDY

A More Human Way of Working
with The Office Group

Situation

Charlie and Ollie are the masterminds behind The Office Group (TOG) and in 2003 they pioneered the concept of shared workspace. Their aim was to reconfigure the modern British workplace to bring it in line with a fast-changing world. They wanted to create beautifully designed buildings that offered great facilities, a variety of space and short-term leases and membership options. It meant that businesses could work and grow in a way that suited them, without having to commit to office space long term.

Challenge

Both with backgrounds in real estate, they had become disillusioned with work space. They didn't feel that it responded to what employees wanted or needed, and they knew that with a little more consideration for the emotional needs of people, they could create vibrant and collaborative working environments that everyone enjoyed working in.

They knew that people wanted a different kind of workplace, but they were lacking choice. Rather than working with the needs of the CEO, they wanted to focus on the needs of employees and believed in doing so that they could create an environment that people would love to be a part of and one that they wouldn't want to leave – especially if it was good value too.

Caring about people was at the core of their philosophy, and they wanted to challenge the way that people worked, moving away from a rigid industry where the landlord was in the driver's seat. They knew that through handing the influence over to the occupier, it would change the way the building worked.

Solution

And it was a success. TOG now has 41 buildings across London with a growing presence in the main UK hubs and Europe. They employ 365 people across their spaces, and they feel they have created a 'family', where fun and friendships are at the heart of the way they work.

The TOG branding is intentionally toned down in all their buildings, as they want members to feel like the space is theirs. It's this lack of 'ego' that has helped them to create a very human and collaborative environment. It's not about TOG; it's about creating beautiful spaces that make others feel happy.

They design their buildings with more open spaces, wider corridors and good levels of natural light, so everyone is close to a window. Members can move freely between the various buildings, which all have their own unique character, and everyone has access to good quality coffee, and on some sites, there are cafes serving nutritious food, gyms, and one even has a clock to time how quickly people make it up the stairs – to encourage them to walk.

The TOG app makes sure that all members can connect with around 50% of TOG members working with other people across the TOG portfolio. They aren't formally introduced – they find each other.

Sustainability has remained a central component of design, and they try to include as many innovations and creative ideas within their designs to inspire green behaviour from staff and members, so that everyone can do their bit.

Outcome

Charlie says they are still as excited about what they do as they were when they started. They love the buzz that comes from creating an amazing building, a great space to work, and then opening the doors and seeing people fill the building up. The 'build it and they will come' sentiment seems particularly apt for TOG, as their occupancy rates have remained high over the years. They have made sure they never got greedy and have continued to focus on what people need – rather than where they can make quick cash. They have remained focused on the end user with the view that if their members put in, they will give it back. They know that everyone has a part to play in making the TOG experience a great one.

They still face challenges, finding the right buildings, the right architects, getting the economics to stack up, which means they can't always open where they want to. They want to resist growth for growth's sake. The TOG business model seems to be working, though, and there is no doubt that it is responding to the evolving world of work.

AWAKE

A Little Recap

When we wake up to who we are as individuals, when we build self knowledge, we can see what is hidden away in our subconscious. It allows us to take better care of ourselves, to make better decisions about how we think and behave, and to help others too.

Conscious intelligence is needed as leaders, to grow ourselves and others to achieve healthier outcomes and performance.

1. There are many dimensions to who we are as people. There are the parts that we know about and are happy for others to know about, and there are parts that are hidden, intentionally or not. When we **seek self-knowledge** and get feedback from those around us, we get to know ourselves better and build on what we do well.
2. We find it hard to live authentically and show our real self to the people around us. Although **we wear masks** to protect ourselves from getting hurt and feeling discomfort, they can affect our long-term happiness and wellbeing.
3. Although we are largely unaware of them, **we are programmed to repeat the patterns** of behaviour and thought that stem from other experiences in our lives. Unless we recognize these patterns, they can negatively affect our performance and wellbeing.
4. **We are often triggered** by the behaviour of those around us, yet most of our reactions are subconscious ones. Through a better of understanding what leads us to experience heightened emotions, we can better regulate our reactions.

5. **We are all biased**, and through becoming more aware of our biases, we can make sure we're not unintentionally having a negative effect on the people around us.

6. Whether we think it or not, **we are always communicating**. Modern day working environments require us to treat others like adults and to be more open and up for two-way dialogue.

7. Often, leaders can be so busy taking a lead in conversations that they fail to realize they are controlling what's being said. Sometimes we need to get out of the way, **take a back seat and listen**, to allow people the space and freedom to speak up and take ownership.

8. Too often, bad behaviour becomes normalized at work because leaders fail to deal with it. When we **stand up to bad behaviour**, we improve wellbeing by putting the needs of the team before any one individual.

9. Our ego and sense of self-importance can undermine the efforts of others. **Leaders must show humility** to achieve the highest levels of performance.

10. Removing the labels assigned to emotions (i.e. positive and negative) and **allowing people to express emotions** constructively leads to greater teamwork and wellbeing.

GROWING

We Need to Grow to Succeed

The Big Conscious Question:
What Else Can I Learn?

Organizations need to grow and develop, and so do people, and unless we're developing people as leaders, we're not being effective. People expect development as part of their psychological contract – the unwritten set of expectations between the employee and the employer.[131] And organizations that support learning and development help employees fulfil two fundamental human needs:[132] the need to be sure we're making progress, and the desire to achieve mastery. In his seminal book about what really motivates us, *Drive*, Dan Pink states that we "have an urge to get better skills".[133] This is why the development of employees is so fundamental to creating a culture of wellbeing.

Employees learn throughout their career so they can function effectively in their roles and leaders can catalyze that learning by providing the right level of support and guidance. The leaders who are really effective don't depend on training and courses to support the learning of their people. They ingrain opportunities for learning in everyday experiences because:

- They believe people can learn and grow
- Failure is seen an inevitable part of life and a great opportunity to learn
- Change is seen an opportunity to learn
- People are encouraged to learn based on their own unique needs
- Learning and mastery is seen as a fundamental human need, not an optional cost-related activity
- They aren't threatened by people becoming better than them – they encourage it
- Everyone is encouraged to learn and grow, not just the more ambitious
- They connect the team to other people with skills and knowledge they don't have

- They encourage experimentation and creativity
- They want to learn themselves and role model learning behaviour

Top-performing organizations are said to be five times more likely to have a learning culture.[134] And the best leaders recognize that simply recruiting the rights skills isn't possible. They must develop talent internally,[135] and they understand that investing time and money in learning and development is simply part of creating good business results and a sustainable organization.

One of the best predictors of employee turnover is the provision of opportunities to learn, grow and advance.[136]

Leaders are perfectly placed to influence the exodus of employees. Rather than running around in a panic to backfill positions of competent and experienced people,[137] focusing on providing the opportunity to learn and develop during an employee's time with the organization is a more effective approach.

Josh Bersin believes the cost of losing an employee can range from tens of thousands of dollars to between one and a half and twice the employee's annual salary. These costs include hiring, on-boarding, training, ramp time to peak productivity, the loss of engagement by others due to high turnover, higher business error rates and general culture impacts.[138]

And although initially most employees are a 'cost' to the organization, over time, with the right support, they become more and more valuable. Leaders who see employees as valuable assets will achieve higher levels of performance in the long term.

Finally, leaders are employees too. When they are growing too, and see learning as a lifelong journey, not one that stops when you become a leader, it positively impacts their results, credibility and long-term performance.

LESSON 34

Effective Leaders Have a Growth Mindset

The role of a leader is to help others to perform. For people to perform at their best, they need to learn. Unless we're learning, we become stagnant and don't improve – that affects our performance and wellbeing. If leaders don't know how to support the development of others, if they don't see it as a fundamental part of their role, they are not being an effective leader.

Unless leaders believe that people can learn, grow and change, and that it can take sustained effort and focus to improve, they will often let their team down. Not because they are bad people, but because the fundamental belief that is driving their behaviour isn't right. From my own experience, the most effective leaders are the ones who invest time and effort in developing others, and who see the value of everyone's untapped potential. There is something that underpins their behaviour, and that is a growth mindset.

Carol Dweck, a Stanford University professor, has spent years researching the concepts of growth and fixed mindsets and their importance in learning. Leaders with a growth mindset believe their talents and those of others can be developed through hard work, good strategies and input from others. Based on that belief, they tend to achieve more than those with a more fixed mindset (who believe their talents are innate gifts). With a growth mindset, we are less bothered about looking smart and more interested in learning. Leaders with a growth mindset are more tolerant and supportive, creating a positive environment in which:

- People can make mistakes – mistakes are a great way to learn
- Thay have realistic expectations of others
- People want to help each other
- People can experiment using different ways of doing things
- The talents of others are embraced
- The leader asks for help
- People are praised for the work they do

In growth mindset companies, leaders express significantly more positive views about their employees than those in fixed-mindset companies, rating them as more innovative, collaborative, and committed to learning and growing. So just by having an orientation towards a growth mindset, leaders feel more positive about their people and are likely to be more motivational.[139]

It takes humility to demonstrate a growth mindset as a leader, and the ability to show vulnerability – something that doesn't always sit well with the role. Leaders that have a fixed mindset often feel the need to protect themselves and their status, and see others as being 'set in their ways' or 'hard to develop'.

A 'pure' growth mindset doesn't exist. We are all a mixture of fixed and growth mindsets, which evolves with time and experience.

It's the extent to which we lean more in one direction or the other that affects how inclined we are as leaders to support the development of others.[140]

Developing a growth mindset can be challenging, and employees need this just as much as leaders do. But we all have fixed-mindset triggers that inhibit the growth mindset, such as facing challenges, receiving criticism, or faring poorly compared with others and falling into insecurity or defensiveness.

This is why some people make little or no progress when they need to improve.[141] Unless people believe they can succeed, they will be stifled, even if they have the capability to do what's being asked of them.

People with a growth mindset actually display different patterns of activation in the brain than those with a fixed mindset. Their mental (attentional) resources are engaged in a way that enhances learning and retention of new information, and they are resilient in the face of setbacks.[142] This is why having a growth mindset is vital for learning, and why such individuals respond better to feedback.

While setbacks and less positive feedback don't always feel good, a growth mindset doesn't seem to create the same kind of anxiety and self-doubt that comes with a fixed mindset.[143] A fixed mindset is often connected with the avoidance of difficult tasks and the fear of failure (which might expose a lack in ability). People with a growth mindset tend to have greater levels of self-esteem and more resilience.

Organizations with a growth mindset culture achieve higher levels of performance because there is more trust and greater ownership, and people are more willing to take risks.[144] Teams with a growth mindset are better at openly expressing disagreements, accepting feedback from one another, learning from challenges and setting more challenging goals for themselves.[145]

How to Foster a Growth Mindset Culture

1. Educate the team – explain growth mindset and the science behind it, so that everyone understands the qualities of both the fixed and growth mindset.
2. Embed growth mindset in performance conversations – during one-to-ones, reviews and career discussions, discuss progress, learning and areas for growth

and development. Try to see mistakes and failures as part of learning and not a reason to blame and persecute.

3. Encourage more risk-taking – knowing that some risks won't work out is all part of learning. People need to be able to experiment, as it's often through trial and error that the best ideas come to the fore. Even if a project does not meet its original goals, ask what went well and what could be even better next time. Use the WWWEBI acronym to frame a look at the lessons learned – What Went Well Even Better If?

Leadership Myths
1. People either have ability or they don't.
2. If they wanted to change, they would.

Get Conscious
Do you believe that attributes are fixed traits that can't be changed, or that they are qualities that can be grown? When someone on the team isn't performing as you would like, do you see it as a development opportunity or a fatal flaw? When you make a mistake, do you try to cover it up? Do you feel you need to look smart? Do you admit to your failings? How do you react when others don't achieve what was hoped for? What triggers you to think from a fixed mindset perspective?

LESSON 35

Focus on What Is Innately Right

In our quest for the highest levels of performance and productivity, we've developed the unenviable ability to spot flaws, notice when things aren't working and point out holes in people's thinking. We've learned that by spotting what's wrong, we can achieve more.

The upside is that we can make improvements if we notice what's not working. The downside is the impact it can have on others. Focusing too heavily in the direction of what's not working or what people aren't achieving can demotivate even the most resilient and confident workforce.[146] An old boss of mine once described it to me as "pushing competence to the point of incompetence". Something I have seen happen numerous times, including to myself.

There are so many examples in the workplace of where we focus on what's wrong, rather than what's right:

1. We 'red pen' people's work, pointing out what needs changing – rather than making comments about what's working well and what could be better.
2. Where someone falls short of achieving a goal, we focus on what's not been done, rather than all of the great progress they've made.
3. When someone moves into a new role and is learning the job, we focus more on what they are getting wrong, rather than noticing where they have made a positive difference.
4. Where someone comes up with a new idea, we point out all the ways in which it might not work, rather than building on the idea to make sure it does.

I could go on.

As humans, we're programmed to look for the negatives and to spot the gaps. Unless we have more of a growth mindset approach or have made a conscious effort to 'be positive', we can focus on what's not working by default. This is especially true when we're under pressure, but it can be demoralizing for those on the receiving end. It often fails to recognize people's strengths, where they've made progress, and the effort that has gone into achieving what they have.

People are motivated by making progress. When we see we have achieved something, it triggers our reward response to release dopamine (a happy hormone), which motivates us to keep going. A leader who recognizes this understands that pointing out what's good, what's working and where people have a strength motivates them to make a continued effort. By highlighting how strengths generate success on the job, employees are motivated to work even harder in these areas, and to produce still more positive behaviours and even better results.[147] A leader who makes a habit of noticing people's strengths can find it easier to have a conversation when it comes to pointing out where improvements are needed, because people will know they are supported and trusted.

An extensive 2016 Gallup study showed that companies achieve better performance when they develop what is innately 'right' with people instead of trying to fix what's 'wrong' with them. Improved sales, profit, customer engagement, turnover, employee engagement and safety are the result.[148]

This isn't only about giving positive feedback and turning a blind eye to anything negative, nor is it about placing people into roles that only play to their strengths. There can be a huge opportunity in developing employees beyond their obvious talents, which is sometimes necessary if they are to perform well in their role. The thing we need to avoid is a default to the negative, or putting people into roles or environments where there is limited opportunity to play to their strengths.

How to Be More Strengths-based

1. Be clear about strengths – help people to understand where they are strong by reinforcing and giving feedback on what they do well, where they excel and where they are making a valued contribution.
2. Organize people's roles around their strengths – understand an individual's strengths, and work with them to shape roles and opportunities that capitalize on them.
3. Give strengths-based feedback – this doesn't mean avoiding what needs improving; that's important too. The key is to become aware of whether your approach is to mainly focus feedback on 'the gap'. If it is, work on getting a better balance of what could make things even better.

Leadership Myths

1. People need to focus on what they don't do well to improve.
2. People understand their own strengths, I don't need to tell them what they are.

Get Conscious

When you look at your team's work, do you tend to focus on what's good or on what's bad? How often do you get frustrated with the performance of a team member, even though you know they aren't playing to their strengths? Do you know what your strengths are? Does your role allow you to play to them? Are you clear about the strengths of your team? Are you capitalizing on those team strengths?

LESSON 36

Feedback as a Normal Everyday Act

If we were only able to do one activity to support people's development, feedback would be one of the top three choices (along with coaching and new developmental experiences). Feedback is one of the most personal and tailored ways of developing others. And it's a wonderful way to build self-knowledge. Yet it can be extremely hard to do well. Very often we deliver feedback in an awkward way, where we give no specifics around the feedback or focus too much on what's wrong. And unless we're clear about what constitutes good performance and have realistic expectations about what people should be achieving, it can be difficult to see when someone is doing well as we don't specifically know what we're assessing their performance against.

Real-time feedback is the only feedback that works effectively, and it requires us to speak to people in the moment or soon after something has happened. We're all subject to recency bias, and if feedback is left, we tend to forget it. So, it's crucial to let people know what you've observed while it's happening.

Very often, when we hold on to feedback, it loses impact. When positive feedback is delayed, we lose the opportunity to build on the positive energy that's been created. And when we hang on to feedback regarding improvements, we can end up being clumsy when we do eventually end up delivering it. That in itself can lead to a delay in delivering the feedback, to the point where the person on the receiving end can't remember the specifics of what happened when you finally get to speak with them. This means they are more likely to be defensive.

Giving feedback in real time not only means that people get to better understand their strengths, and where they are adding value, but it also allows for ongoing course correction, limiting rework and keeping people focused on where they can have the biggest impact. To provide better real-time feedback, leaders need to understand themselves better. That's because our beliefs, our standards and the relationships we have with our team significantly influence how we give feedback.

Unless we have a growth mindset, we tend to default to giving negative feedback, which is not going to lead to motivated, high-performing individuals. Only when we believe that someone can improve and grow do we tend to give feedback in a supportive and forward-looking way. With a growth mindset, we give balanced feedback that focuses on strengths and areas for improvement. We are more likely to see the value of failure and setbacks, using them as a good opportunity for learning and growth.

The standards we set, and our expectations of others, significantly influence our approach to feedback and our recognition of where people are doing a good job. Leaders who expect a lot from themselves will often have exceptionally high and unrealistic standards for the team. So, they will tend to provide good feedback only when people have delivered what they see as exceptional performance, and tend to default to spotting flaws. The fact is that leaders with high standards tend to be overly critical when it comes to reviewing other's performance, but as I've already suggested, too much negative feedback doesn't motivate anyone. If your standards are unrealistically high (or if you tend to be critical of yourself), finding good in the work of others will simply be a lot harder.

If you don't have a good relationship with others and don't spend enough time with them to know whether they are doing a good job, giving feedback can become even

THE **CONSCIOUS** EFFECT

more difficult. Even if you don't work closely with people, your role as leader is to stay connected, so that the 'partnership' between you and the people you lead remains strong.

When you do give feedback, make sure it's specific. People need to know exactly why something is good, valuable or needs improving. Too often managers say, 'You're doing a great job' or 'I have no problems with your performance', yet that gives no guidance to someone about what they need to improve or where they are making the biggest difference.

Use teachable moments. If you feel an individual could have done better, ask them in the moment what they thought went well and what could be better next time. By raising awareness in the moment, people can better understand the context and reflect on how they should improve for the future.

Finally, all feedback should be given with kindness. As long as people know you have their best interests at heart, they are more likely to respond well to what you have to say.

How to Build a Real-time Feedback Culture

1. Notice progress – once people know where they should be or want to head, and once everyone is clear about the focus for performance, it is much easier to notice when progress is being made. Make sure you point out where people are doing well and use 'teachable' moments to chat through areas for improvement.
2. Stay in real time – make feedback a normal and natural part of everyday discussions. Feedback doesn't only have to come from leaders; organizations with a culture of openness are more likely to share feedback across teams and departments.
3. Build strong partnerships – leaders who work harder on having relationships and connecting with their team

206

will be able to have more open and honest conversations, where people feel less threatened.

Leadership Myths

1. It's fine to leave feedback until the annual review.
2. The feedback sandwich works – improvement feedback sandwiched between positive feedback (people see through it).

Get Conscious

Do you give much feedback? Do you notice where your people are doing a good job? Do you mention it to them? Do you point out the specifics of why and how they are doing well? When you notice where things need improving, are you able to talk about it in a supportive way? What stops you? Have you ever worked with someone who was good at giving feedback? What made them effective? How do you feel about receiving feedback yourself? Is that impacting your ability to provide it to others?

LESSON 37

Underperformance Is Often Environmental

Leaders often get frustrated by the performance of individuals. Many call HR in for help, to either get the person to work more effectively or, depending on the situation, to remove them from the organization. Unfortunately, where targets need to be met and performance needs to be optimized, some leaders have little time and patience for someone who isn't 'pulling their weight'.

More often than not, when an individual isn't performing as they should be, it's the environment around them that's the problem, not their will or capability. Unfortunately, leaders often blame the individual for the underperformance.

Our natural aversion to having difficult conversations can make these situations worse, and allow underperformance to continue for some time. As time lapses, the problem grows, and what could initially have been a quick and straightforward conversation can lead to a more serious performance issue.

So if an individual's will and capability haven't led to the problem, it's important to understand what has. According to Rose Mueller-Hanson and Elaine Pulakos, authors of the book *Transforming Performance Management to Drive Performance*,[149] "a critical first step in managing poor performance is to carefully diagnose its root cause". Many powerful factors sit outside the employee's control, and so the environment they are in can have a big impact on them. The list of environmental factors influencing employees' performance is long. Policies and procedures, uncooperative colleagues, structures that inhibit communication, culture, lack of resources, poorly designed workflows and processes, workload or tasks not appropriate for the employee's role: these all play a part.[150]

Although a lack of will or low capability may be causing the problem, it is not helpful to default to identifying these as the primary reasons. Leaders must assess whether the working environment could be contributing to underperformance, because otherwise the employee may be treated unfairly and criticized. This can lead to a negative impact on mental health. Simply changing the conditions around an employee can sometimes help to make the improvements required.

When an individual's will is the issue, leaders should try to identify and understand the underlying problem that is causing the underperformance. By being more curious, leaders are more likely to find out what's really going on, and often a simple conversation with the individual can reveal the cause of the problem.

When it comes to capability issues, leaders should be giving clear feedback and developing their people, not leaving them to flounder. Sometimes employees simply aren't clear about what is expected of them, and there may be a disconnect between what the employee thinks they need to do and what the leader wants.

When reviewing performance, it helps leaders if they understand that 'people are doing the best with the resources that they have'. No one wants to come to work and do a bad job. Most people are doing their best based on the knowledge, direction, understanding, tools and energy they have at their disposal. By thinking in this way, leaders can assess the problem more compassionately and objectively, and take a more productive and sensible approach to solving the problem.

One final point to remember is that personal problems impact people's performance. Personal problems can lead to distractions or be the cause of mental health problems, and they vary in duration. In these situations, leaders can help by creating a space to speak openly about problems and signpost people towards the right support.

How to Help People with Their Performance
1. Avoid blame – look at the environment and be honest about what may be getting in the way of better performance. It's often easier to blame the individual even when it's not their fault.
2. Clarify expectations – sometimes there's a breakdown in communication or understanding. Define goals, be clear about the scope of the role and describe your expectations about the outcomes you're expecting.
3. Provide support – don't expect employees to perform well all of the time. If something doesn't seem right, show compassion, use coaching to help them and give them the space to make improvements.

Leadership Myths
1. People tend to know when they're not doing a good enough job.
2. Poor performance is always down to the individual.

Get Conscious
When someone isn't doing what you need from them, do you automatically blame them? Do you ever look at the environment they are working in? Do you ever ask the team what they need to work more effectively (what's blocking the best performance)? Do you default to blame when someone isn't working well? Do you work in 'partnership' with the individual to solve the problem? Do you see your team's performance as a reflection of your own performance? If not, why not?

LESSON 38

Appraisals Are Dead.
Long Live Conversations

The annual appraisal is a staple activity of many organizations, yet it's an unsatisfying process for most of us. Employees can be surprised by feedback if it's only provided annually in an appraisal and keeping goals relevant when they are set and reviewed once a year simply isn't realistic. That's why they often haven't been done by the time an individual's review comes around. The whole process, if done annually, isn't very human and isn't very effective.

'Performance management' is an awful term too. It conjures up images of whip-cracking and critical judgments of others – that's probably because often that's exactly what it is. Or it's a skewed conversation as employees try to convey the best possible view, knowing their review will impact their pay review, bonus or promotion. Rather than motivating employees, the annual appraisal ends up being a tick-box exercise focused on all the wrong things. They are long-winded and backward-looking, when all employees really want to do is look forward and focus on how they can do a better job.

When we review performance continually, it becomes more human and a part of day-to-day operations. Continuous performance management (or development) means having shorter, more informal conversations (check-ins) about performance and development, setting agile goals that can be adapted and flexed. And rather than being a time when feedback is given, because that is happening in real time as and when it's needed, the check-in becomes a time when feedback is reviewed, and progress is discussed. Having more regular conversations, with a greater focus on individual development, what's going well, and where the individual can have the greatest impact, is far more relevant and motivating. When performance management is continuous, it's not an HR process but an important operational process that keeps employees and leaders connected and looking forward to what needs to happen next. When this happens, it leads to:

- Greater awareness and honest discussion about the constraints and barriers to good performance, e.g. processes, resources, support, etc.
- Shared responsibility between employees and managers
- Real-time analysis of results so that issues can be spotted and corrected early
- A focus on meaningful conversations rather than paperwork
- Goal-setting that is linked to the needs of the individual, the team and the organization as they evolve

How to Manage Performance Well

1. Focus on development – you can focus on task completion day to day, using check-ins to discuss goals, development and progress.
2. Focus on the future – neuroscience has proven that understanding progress is what drives performance and is often more motivational that the achievement of goals. A focus on progress changes the dynamic of employees receiving judgment from managers to a dialogue that covers how things are going, what is getting in the way of progress and how any barriers can be removed.
3. Set and flex goals – set near-term goals (three to five) and review these regularly. It motivates people and keeps performance focused in the right way (see Chapter 47: Goals Keep Us Focused).

Leadership Myths

1. Goals should be set once a year.
2. The annual appraisal is when feedback should be given.

Get Conscious

How effectively does your performance management approach work? How often do you discuss people's development and progress in comparison to operational delivery? How could you incorporate more regular conversations in to daily operations? Do you set flexible objectives that can be adapted throughout the year? Do you see appraisals/reviews as a chance for you tell someone how they are doing or as an opportunity for a two-way discussion?

LESSON 39

Leaders Who 'Know Nothing' Are Better

Some of you will have been on coaching courses or experienced models such as GROW (Goals, Reality, Obstacles, Will). These models are useful for understanding the principles of coaching and give a structure for a full coaching conversation, but coaching – at its core – is about getting curious and asking good questions. If you do it effectively, you will take a 'know nothing' approach, which means asking questions without judgment or the need to provide the answers.

It may sound straightforward, but it's not. Most of us are used to solving problems or giving advice. Coaching goes against what we are naturally programmed to do. Yet asking good questions can lead to the most brilliant discoveries and allows others to find solutions for themselves. Coaches know that simply by asking questions, it taps into an individual's subconscious, creating new thinking and releasing what's already there. When we ruminate on problems or try to come up with ideas in our own heads, we can go around in circles. It's distracting and can start a pattern of thoughts that hinders our thinking and clouds our judgment.

A well-placed question creates a more conscious awareness and can help us view the problem from a new perspective. The beauty of being asked questions by others is that they're often questions we haven't asked ourselves and even if we have considered them before, speaking out loud tends to give us greater clarity. We stop playing the same narrative in our head. It puts a 'wedge' in our current thinking.

When a coach is skilled, they are able to share insights and play back what they are hearing from the individual being coached. This allows that individual to deepen their self-knowledge and consider the reality of what they are saying and their thinking. Coaching takes practice, and the more you practise as a coach, the better you get at asking good questions.

Coaching leads to a number of benefits for the coachee. It can help them to:

- solve their own problems
- take ownership and more control over outcomes
- create the motivation to take action
- achieve greater insights and understanding into their problems
- become more self-aware
- make decisions that suit their own individual circumstances
- be less dependent on others

Coaching is a brilliant tool for helping people to focus, for gaining perspective and for boosting confidence. Often, when a leader starts to coach their people, they find themselves wanting to jump in and give the answers, or steer the coachee in a certain direction. However, the more you practise and see how effective others are at solving their own problems, the less likely you are to do this. Coaching helps the individual (the coachee), but it also helps the leader (the coach). Although it may seem that coaching is time-consuming, getting others to think for themselves breaks the dependency they have on you. In the long term, it's a time saver.

Leaders can benefit from coaching too. Leadership can be a very lonely role, and given the pressures and conflicting priorities leaders face, having a coach can help them keep a clear head – often there are coaches in the organization who will help. Coaching is a highly personalized type of development that enables a leader to stay focused. With the support of a coach, a leader can start to explore sides of themselves they may not be familiar with and increase their self-knowledge, interpersonal skills and impact as a leader.

How to Develop Your Coaching Capabilities

1. Ask more questions – although it may take some getting used to, for you and the team, asking more questions will encourage people to come up with the answers for themselves.
2. Stop answering questions – even though sometimes you will need to provide the answers, try asking individuals what they think instead when they come to you with a question. It may take them time to get used to, but they will start thinking for themselves soon enough.
3. Explore problems – often we hear about a problem and go into 'solution mode'. All problems need a solution, and the quicker we find one, the quicker we can move on. But that doesn't always lead to the best solution and it minimizes learning. Instead of jumping in, probe the problem. Find out more about it, ask more questions, and get others involved in finding the solution.

Leadership Myths

1. My job is to tell people what to do.
2. I haven't got time to coach.

Get Conscious

How many questions do you ask? When there is a problem to solve, how likely are you to get curious and ask questions using a 'know nothing' approach? How easy is it for you be quiet while other people figure out the answers? How likely are you to jump in when someone is answering a question?

LESSON 40

Learn, Unlearn and Relearn

Early in our careers, we spend most of our time learning. We'll have recently finished our education, where learning was a big part of our life, and when we join the workforce we develop new skills and learn about how it all works or how to behave as an effective team member. Learning is an essential and normal part of what we do.

Then there's a shift. As we progress in our careers, very often we reach a point where we become so knowledgeable and experienced that we forget or stop trying to actively learn. We often don't notice this happening, but we become more confident in our knowledge and experience, so we no longer seek learning, and we stagnate. Any growth that happens tends to be towards our technical and professional skills. We neglect personal development and areas in which we can benefit from growing emotionally and behaviourally.

When we stop learning, it impacts our performance. When we stop reading, attending conferences, joining new networks, listening, asking questions or training, we narrow our field of vision. It means we become dependent on the knowledge we've built up over the years. This isn't good for our own performance or that of the team.

Learning isn't just about learning what's new to us. As our knowledge and experience grows and our organizations change, we sometimes have to unlearn what we previously depended on. This doesn't mean deleting old knowledge, as there is little evidence to suggest that we can do that. It means changing the meaning we've previously given to something, or no longer using specific information if we know it's wrong or less effective than something else. Confirmation bias makes us hold onto misbeliefs for a long time, as we unconsciously seek information to prove, through rationalization, what we believe to be right or true. This is why behavioural change can be quite tough. But by raising our conscious awareness, we can wilfully and unconsciously change the importance we place on pretty much everything that we think and believe.[151]

The ability to continually learn and challenge old beliefs, assumptions and knowledge is essential for a leader. It helps us to continue innovating and prevents us from holding others back with antiquated ideas and reference points. Leaders who believe they can take their foot off the 'learning gas' when they reach the higher echelons couldn't be further from the truth. This is where the most difficult learning starts, as we have to learn more about ourselves and each other – and this is complicated. It's the Conscious Intelligence I spoke about earlier in the book.

Leaders need to see learning as a sign of great role modelling and humility, and not as a sign of weakness. Good leaders develop through continuously learning about their personalities, relationships and careers, and the kind of leader they want to become. A sign of a good leader is one with a passion about excelling and a dedication to achieving this through continual learning.[152]

Learning is not always easy, especially if we haven't done it for a while. So we convince ourselves that we're fine, that we have the necessary knowledge, and we carry on regardless. According to Bradley Staats, in his book *Never Stop Learning*,[153] becoming "a dynamic learner is not a one-step process". It's about how "we incorporate failure, ask questions, reflect, play to our strengths and learn from others".

It's the same for our people.[154] Expecting them to get most of what they need from a classroom environment is unrealistic. There are opportunities to learn every day, through new experiences, feedback, reviewing lessons learned, asking others for input and by staying connected to people who can coach and mentor.

Relearning is also important, especially for entrepreneurs who rediscover old skills and strengths when they leave paid employment. It's not about starting from scratch. It's like dusting off an old pair of boots and polishing them up. The knowledge is still there; we just need to bring it back to our conscious awareness and get it polished up.

How to Learn More

1. Ask for feedback – a great method, because we have as much to learn about ourselves, and how effective we are, as we do about our subject matter. Research shows that the most effective leaders regularly ask for feedback.[155]
2. Speak to your team – insights from team members can expand the knowledge of leaders, especially in a culture where team members are empowered to seek out new knowledge and information.
3. Broaden your network – this avoids becoming too internally focused and provides the opportunity to hear the latest thinking around your areas of interest. It also provides the chance to meet others you can collaborate with.

Leadership Myths

1. I did all of my development when I was younger.
2. My knowledge has got me this far, and it's good enough.

Get Conscious

What do you do to add to your learning? Do you question your current thinking or ideas, or stay open minded when others do this? Are you role modelling the behaviour you want your team to be demonstrating in relation to learning? What gets in the way of you expanding your knowledge and skills? Could you overcome those challenges?

LESSON 41

Learning Human Skills

The Fourth Industrial Revolution is upon us, and the way we work is shifting. Though this is definitely not my area of expertise, it would be remiss of me not to cover it, given its potential effects on the way that we work. Technology is changing the way we do things, with developments like artificial intelligence (AI), mobile platforms and social collaboration systems creating an abundance of opportunities for organizations to improve the way they work.

Anthony Slumbers travels the globe speaking about how technology is redefining how we work, shop and live, and the opportunities and threats of our changing world. He explained to me that "we are moving to a world where many of our tasks at work are going to be automated", and directed me to a report by McKinsey that suggests that 49% of the activities that people are paid to do in the global economy have the potential to be automated.[156]

Although this presents opportunities to improve productivity and connectivity, there is also the down side of job losses. Although there are competing views on this, with some saying that more jobs will be created, unless we reskill people, job losses are inevitable.

Anthony talked to me about the skill set we will need in the future and referred to it as "human stuff". And this human stuff is about the work that only humans can really do. It involves design, imagination, inspiration, creation, empathy, intuition, innovation, collaboration, social intelligence and judgment.[157] All of these things require the high-level reasoning that only humans can perform.

We will need to better utilize our human skills while learning to interface with the technology that will surround us. This is why training and education will have to be a top priority and building Conscious Intelligence will play an even more important part in our performance. It won't be a case of whether you need to have technical or human skills, as people will need both.

As we move in to an era where humans + machines = superpowers,[158] we enter a world where human empowerment is truly possible, and the opportunity for more 'good work' that we enjoy more is a very real possibility.[159]

How to Build Skills for the Future

1. Get clear – and review your team and organization to understand the impact of the revolution. Have you got the right skills for the future?
2. Develop human skills – by identifying the potential impact, leaders can start to assess which roles, or parts of roles, are likely to be affected. They should think about how to develop the higher reasoning capabilities required for the next decade, skills that could also enable them to perform better in the short term too.
3. Develop technical skills – people will have to take responsibility for spotting the opportunities that technology can bring. This means having the right level of technical capability in the organization. These individuals will need human skills too, given the interplay between technology and people.[160]

Leadership Myths

1. Our people won't be too affected by technological advances.
2. Humans already know how to be effective humans.

Get Conscious

Are you thinking about the impacts of this revolution on your organization? Are you considering the impact on people? If not, why not? Do you think your people might be concerned about how it is going to impact them? Are you dealing with potential anxiety in the workforce? Do you expect that you will simply 'lose heads' when the time comes? Are you doing anything to develop 'human skills' now?

LESSON 42

Find the Best People, Then Let Them Go

The relationships employees have with an employer should start when they are looking for a job and last until well after they've left.

It is hard to find great talent. It is an ongoing challenge. What has changed dramatically over time is how we find that talent, and how they find us as employers. In the past, recruitment agencies would put posters in their windows and place adverts in newspapers to attract people. And it worked, without too much effort. The good old days.

Nowadays, LinkedIn is the go-to tool for recruitment consultants to 'mine' people out of their jobs, often before the individuals have even decided they want to leave. A prospective candidate is likely to use sites like Glassdoor to seek reviews about the company's CEO, and social media is used to check corporate responsibility credentials and values. There are so many touch points between organizations and candidates that organizations are having to invest significantly more time and effort into making sure they 'appear well' in the market.

Employers are having to pay more attention than ever to their brand and to the candidate experience in order to attract good people. Selection processes are also becoming slicker, honed to make sure bias is minimized, with more focus being put on behavioural 'fit' and attracting ever more diverse pools of talent.

Yet how many recruitment processes help us to get to the heart of who people really are, as opposed to what they can do?

Most organizations are focused on an individual's skills, their previous experience and their personality. Yet how do we know we're going to have a good relationship with the person if they join? How do we know if their values match ours? And how do we know what really excites them, and what brings out their best? What are their real strengths – when they often won't know themselves?

By finding out what is important to people, what motivates them, what they are doing when they have their best day at work and what makes them happy, and their values, we get a deeper understanding of the individual and can recognize if they will 'fit' the organization. There is a better chance of these individuals enjoying what they do when they join, staying engaged with the purpose of the organization and feeling they can add value. This means getting better at asking questions that dig out this information to make sure the right people are joining us based on better quality information.

And once they've joined us, and spent some time doing great work for us and growing, we need to get better at letting them go too and keeping the relationships alive into the future.

When people hand in their notice, for whatever reason, leaders can take it personally, seeing it as a sign of failure on their part or disloyalty on the part of the individual. Reactions can range from leaders ignoring people, to asking them to leave straightaway (restrictive covenants can have an impact on this), to holding them to unrealistic notice periods when the individual has already 'checked out'. Sometimes we even convince people to stay, only to find they leave a few months later. Many of these management reactions are fundamentally wrong.

Unfortunately, leaders often see an employment contract like a marriage. Once you're in, you're committed for life, 'till death do us part'. They don't see the value in someone going off to explore other opportunities, and the value that will have for their growth and development.

They become selfish and see a leaver as a problem they have to deal with.

As the gig economy enables more flexibility in the workplace and gives people a chance for portfolio careers and to work wherever and whenever they want, leaders will need to get to grips with employing a more fluid and independent workforce.

This is just like a teenager heading off to university. A parent may struggle with seeing them leave but by letting them go, they can allow them to flourish and become even better people.

A company with a refreshing approach to employees leaving is Innocent Drinks. Their offices are fantastic, filled with green artificial grass, Lego walls, and dispersed teams who sit wherever they want. When people decide to leave, they create a smoothie bottle label for every 'alumni' member who has worked for them. They print their unique 'ingredients' list on the label, and these are showcased on the walls of the office so that everyone who has worked for Innocent Drinks is enshrined and remembered for their unique contribution. They have a wall celebrating the success of previous employees, with the businesses they've opened and the products they've developed on display for all to see too. Along the staircases there is a timeline of the company's history, with the people involved in developing the company there too. They have a positive mindset about leavers. I'm sure it's not always easy to see people go but by celebrating their time with the company, they help to make the leaving process more positive. They are proud of the people who have worked for them and want to continue celebrating them after they've left – and the difference they made. They don't expect people to stay with them for life. They want them to come in and contribute something amazing; when the time is right, they celebrate their departure and the next stage on their journey.

How to Say Hello and Goodbye Better

1. Publish a clear 'why' – anything that prospective candidates can see in the market about an employer must create a compelling reason as to why they should join. Make it clear what you stand for, what you're trying to achieve, why you do what you do and why they would want to work for you. This way you are more likely to attract people who buy into the philosophy of the organization.

2. Do human recruitment – find out who people really are. Get rid of the old questions like 'What are your strengths?' and 'Where do you see yourself in five years?'. Ask deeper questions like these: What is the best day you've ever had at work and why? What gets you out of bed in the morning? How do you find meaning in your work? What are the values that guide you at work? What do you expect from your teammates? Who was the best leader you've ever had? What made them great? What brings out your best? What excites you about life? What are your long term ambitions? What's on your bucket list? What makes you happy?

3. Party when people leave – when someone wants to leave, make it a celebration. Talk about the difference the person has made, why it's been great to have them with the organization. And find ways to remember them and stay connected. Focus on the legacy they will be leaving, not the gap.

Leadership Myths

1. Interviewing is about technical skills and competence.
2. When someone resigns, they are being disloyal.

Get Conscious

When you're recruiting, do you try to find out who the person really is? Do you put too much focus on their technical capability? Do you end up with an understanding of their values and what truly motivates them at work? Do you feel wounded when people resign? Do you listen to their feedback in order to make improvements to the environment? Do you make them feel good about the contribution they've given to the organization?

CASE STUDY

Being Different
with Pure Planet

Situation

Pure Planet is the UK's first app-based energy supplier. Launched in 2017, it is driven by a vision to help create a world powered by clean, green, affordable renewables. Its clean electricity and carbon offset gas are cheaper for householders than traditional 'dirty' equivalents.

Challenge

Pure Planet does innovative work, and so it wanted to do things differently in the workplace too. It offers its team a green-only car policy, bike-to-work scheme and an ethical, sustainable pension scheme. It's a signatory to the UN's Global Compact, supports the Sustainable Development Goals, and is a Living Wage and Disability Confident employer. It wanted to create a working environment where people could easily share ideas and collaborate, where there were minimal rules, and where work fitted around people's lives and not the other way around. It also wanted to give people more choice over how they worked. By doing this, they would have happier people, higher productivity and better people.

Solution

A principle that drove most of the decisions about how Pure Planet would work was 'trust and equality' – everybody would be entitled to the same benefits. Every employee is in the staff share-option scheme, giving them a 'piece' of Pure Planet.

The founders knew that by trusting their people and giving them more choice and flexibility in how they work, it would create an environment where people were empowered and motivated. It has led to a number of ways of working:

1. Purpose – everyone is very engaged with the purpose of the company, which is to create a Britain powered entirely by affordable renewables. They can see how their role directly impacts on this purpose, and this gives them the ability to give something back.

2. Flexible working – people can work wherever they want without feeling guilty, and many people choose to work in the office because of the social benefits. There are very few guidelines, although everyone needs to be in for the team meeting once a month.

3. Unlimited holiday – a minimum of 25 days, and if employees need more, they just have to ask.

4. Equal parental leave – Pure Planet was the first (and remains the only) energy supplier in Britain to offer all its staff, regardless of gender, exactly the same rights and financial benefits whenever they have a child through birth, surrogacy or adoption.

5. Communication – keeping everyone connected is important, and so they use various communication channels, including Slack, and the monthly team meetings.

6. Open and honest environment – people are encouraged to speak the truth, suggest new ideas or call out things that need to improve. There's an informal way of working, no hierarchy, and people can get involved in projects beyond their immediate role.

7. Functional teams – based on the work being done and the skills needed to do it. There is a 'head' for each functional team, and their role is to get the best out of colleagues on behalf of members. In member services, they have a rolling

team leader that changes every six months, and the person who was acting as leader goes back to their original role. They spend 50% of their time in a customer-facing role, and 50% of their time looking after their fellow team members. This gives them the opportunity to develop new skills such as leadership, decision-making and wider problem-solving.

8. No annual appraisal – instead employees work with functional heads to set objectives that are regularly reviewed through one-to-ones. Separate personal developmental meetings happen as needed, at least every three months.

9. Principles not policies - Pure Planet has as few policies as possible (beyond those that are legally required). The expenses policy, for instance, is simply: "Claim what is fair and genuine; no more, no less."

10. No formal job descriptions – there is a one pager setting out a handful of expectations for each role. Within reason, people are expected to be dynamic and adapt to what's needed to get the work done.

Outcome

This has led to is a 100% satisfaction score for Pure Planet from the rapidly expanding team, for each of the last three six-monthly team surveys. The company has also been a winner or finalist in several awards as the 'best place to work'. At the time of writing, it has 100% scores and five stars on Glassdoor.

It is not always easy finding solutions that work for everyone, though. For the customer service team, for instance, totally flexibility over hours was hard to achieve. So Pure Planet created other ways to provide flexibility and make sure people on that team weren't disadvantaged. The company also has to be mindful when people join, as they may not be used to working in such a flexible way. This means helping people to acclimatize to a 'freer' way of working.

CASE STUDY

Creating Unity
with Arcadis

Situation

Arcadis is a global design and consulting firm. They employ 28,000 people across 70 countries. Over the last few years, they have made a number of mergers and acquisitions all over the world. This led to them rebranding the business and bringing the growing and diverse range of people they employed together under one single brand, creating a stronger, more integrated global business.

Challenge

As part of the branding project, they wanted to make sure they clearly defined how everyone should work together and with clients, giving everyone a unified sense of purpose and a common operating system. Putting people first (one of their values) was at the heart of the transformation agenda, and they created a clear vision to 'improve quality of life'. The challenge was to help everyone understand the part they played in bringing the vision to life and get the workforce working together in the same direction.

Solution

An extensive change programme has enabled them to start working towards realizing their vision:

1. A 'Grow, Perform, Succeed' performance development system – where Arcadis set up a series of objectives with their people at the start of the year. Some are role-specific, and some are behavioural and associated with personal development. Line managers are encouraged to give real-time feedback and to meet with employees at informal bi-monthly quality touchpoints to review progress, refocus goals, receive feedback and celebrate success. This assures there are no surprises at the annual review.

2. Being the Best behavioural framework – which embodies the values and core behaviours. People know what is expected of them, and are recognised and rewarded accordingly – with objectives and reviews linking clearly to these expectations. People are encouraged to give and seek feedback around the framework.

3. Leadership framework – to give senior leaders very clear expectations that are included in a balanced scorecard made up of seven behavioural attributes. As well as numerical, hard measures linked to delivery in the role, behaviours are seen as equally important when reviewing performance.

4. Agile working – all vacancies are available as part-time roles to ensure the best pool of talent and to be flexible around people's needs. Their workplace blueprint is designed to foster collaboration and creativity, and stops people working in silos. All key offices are designed in the same consistent way, with 'change champions' used to manage the office moves. Very few people have a permanent desk, as it's important that people can flex and move around – working from home or offsite when they need to.

5. Diversity and inclusion focus – with all leaders receiving training on unconscious bias, including a series of activities to ensure that D&I are being openly talked

about, with people actively encouraged to be their true selves.

6. Mental health awareness – working with MIND to remove the stigma of mental health issues and to better support those with challenges. Mental health first aiders have been trained all around the business.

7. Career framework – so for every discipline strand there is a clear role description and a set of expectations at each level. The steps required to move up through the business are very clear. This information is available to everyone and gives people the opportunity to better own their development.

8. Achieving balance – with leaders encouraged not to communicate outside of office hours and everyone actively discouraged from working at weekends. Annual leave is monitored to make sure that people are taking time off.

Outcome

It's early days, but having been to the Arcadis offices myself, it's obvious people seem enthused by the changes, especially the flexible way in which everyone is encouraged to work. They have seen improvements in attrition and productivity, and the culture is changing, too. Richard Bonner, the company's UK Property MD, has been with the company for 12 years. He explained that the organization is now much more open and transparent. He believes this openness has contributed to bringing people together, and said, "When you're able to be clear about where you're going, what your motivators are as a business and the expectations you have of individuals, it creates an environment for people for thrive."

GROWING

A Little Recap

Creating a culture of learning means establishing the mindset and processes that best support people to learn and grow. Developing others is a fundamental part of a leader's role and by understanding what brings out the best in people, more effective steps can be taken to support learning.

1. **Leaders need a growth mindset** to support others to develop effectively. Growth mindset individuals believe their success is based on hard work and learning and see failure as an opportunity for growth. Just knowing about growth and fixed mindsets can improve your ability to learn.
2. A focus on **individual strengths boosts performance**. By understanding what we do well, we can repeat what is working well. Our reward system is also triggered when we do well and receive positive feedback, and this motivates us to perform better.
3. People can develop and focus their efforts better when **real-time feedback** is integrated into everyday conversations.
4. Leaders may think underperformance is about the will or capability of an individual, but it is the **working environment that has the biggest impact on performance**.
5. When leaders focus more on **regular check-ins to discuss development** and progress, performance accelerates.
6. **Coaching is central to the development of individuals**. This ability to question is a core skill for leaders to grow others and empower them to take ownership.

7. The most successful leaders continue to learn throughout their career. As well as new knowledge, and self-knowledge, **'unlearning' is also an important aspect** of a leader's learning journey.

8. The Fourth Industrial Revolution will see workplaces needing to place greater **focus on developing human skills** involving higher reasoning.

9. We are in relationship with people before and after they join us. We need to get better at **knowing people before they join us and celebrating them when they leave**.

PURPOSEFUL

Organizations
That Build Success
Together Thrive

The Big Conscious Question:
Why Am I Doing This?

Organizations are made up of a series of relationships that come together for the success of the venture – employees, customers, suppliers, communities, regulators, investors – they all have a role to play in achieving success. When employees are in a relationship with an organization, they are working for something that is greater than themselves. This means contributing in a meaningful way to achieve success, both individually and as part of the whole. When we know we are making a valuable contribution and when our work matters, it contributes to the way we feel and to our wellbeing.

When leaders are clear about what everyone is working towards and why it's important, it helps to organize efforts in a coherent way. This means that everyone who interfaces with the organization is more likely to understand the role that they play in creating success and where to prioritize their efforts.

Through being clear about why an organization does what it does, it provides a clear focus. For individuals and for policies and procedures, systems and operational practices. They can all evolve underpinned by clear principles that unite them.

Organizations get confused or lose focus when a clear framework has not been set in place: a plan of purpose, values, beliefs, work practices, policies. They presume people will turn up and know how to work, where to focus, and how to 'be' with each other. This leads to confusion, conflict and relationship breakdowns, as people make assumptions about how the organization works and why their efforts matter. Yet when an organization gives clear guidance on its existence – its purpose – it moves people in the same direction.[161]

There is growing evidence of the link between a clear purpose and better results,[162] with research showing that purposeful brands outperform those without a clear purpose by 133%.[163] In fact, 90% of executives surveyed agree that commitment to purpose-driven leadership produces long-term financial benefits.[164]

Purpose helps organizations to focus on the meaning behind their actions, and the contribution they are making not just to the people they employ, but to customers and society too. And when an organization can articulate and demonstrate the positive difference it is making, it builds trust. Given that only 52% of people are said to trust businesses to do the right thing,[165] that building of trust is important. It affects people's decisions about whether to work for an organization and whether to buy from them. It affects the bottom line. In numerous studies, purposeful organizations achieve better outcomes.

- Employee engagement rises to 73% from 23% in purposeful organizations[166]
- When considering a new job, 79% of people think about a business's social and environmental commitments[167]
- 34% of leaders believe that purpose is a guide for leadership decision-making[168]
- Millennials are 5.3 times more likely to stay with an employer when they connect to the purpose; non-millennials are 2.3 times more likely to stay[169]
- 91% of consumers will switch to a purpose-driven brand of similar price and quality[170]

This is why organizations like A Blueprint for Better Business exist. They see the benefits that purpose brings, and they believe in a better way of doing business. Their ambition is to work with businesses as a force for good, wanting more businesses to operate towards a purpose that respects people while contributing to a better society.

They believe that by doing this, businesses can deliver long-term sustainable performance, because respect for people and giving them an opportunity to contribute to a better society are foundational in building the relationships that underpin and drive successful ventures.

Justin Varney, who works for Business in the Community, a UK-based business-community outreach charity, agrees. He believes that business can create a positive and sustainable community by being at the heart of it and says that one of the most efficient ways to do this is by using purposeful leadership at every level of the organization. Although Justin sees the disconnect between what some leaders say and what they do in reality, there are a number of employers who are using their voice in society to talk about and improve societal issues like water pollution, mental health, the global supply chain, modern slavery and urbanization. 'Conscious leaders' see problems as 'our issue and not their issue', explicitly thinking about the team, co-creation, and what is going to work for everyone, inside and outside of the organization, rather than simply focusing on commercial gains.

It's this focus on relationships and higher purpose that leads to conscious business: the triple bottom line of people, profit and planet.[171]

LESSON 43

Our Search for Meaning

According to John Hutton, the Head of Sustainability at BAM Nuttall, staff want to be encouraged, inspired, feel happy, feel like they are contributing, and working towards a purposeful goal and the greater good.[172] There is increasing evidence that shows that people want purpose and use this a criterion for selecting a new employer.[173]

As humans we come ready-made with a sense of purpose. People want meaning in their lives; it contributes to our wellbeing, and working for an organization that has a sense of meaning enables that. When an organization has a strong sense of why it does what it does – a purpose – it helps people to focus their efforts and to understand the contributions they are making to the company, as well as society.[174]

In *Drive*, Dan Pink described how companies with a transcendent purpose truly ignite spirit in their people.[175] This is purpose with a capital 'P'. He has since gone on to talk about purpose with a small 'p'. When people know that they are making a contribution, either at a local or global level, it makes a difference to the way they feel. Research has shown that by contributing to a higher purpose, people have a healthier outlook on life and even become more resistant to stress.[176] It's because purpose gives us energy that drives us forward.

Many organizations may think they have a purpose and a set of values that are embedded; yet many only have a pipe-dream on a wall somewhere. When purpose is truly embodied, it creates a shared energy, aligns thinking and efforts, and gets people to work collaboratively for the greater good. Purpose needs to be brought to life in the services we offer, the decisions we make, the way we are structured, the way we communicate, the way we behave, the policies we create and the way that we lead.

According to a PwC survey, the top three priorities for employees are: meaning in day-to-day work; a strong sense of community; and feeling energized by knowing the company's impact. Interestingly, for leaders the results are slightly different. They prioritize reputation for growth and innovation, and being seen as distinct and different.[177] This disparity could be leading to the lack of employee engagement and productivity that we see today. All of these things are no doubt important for organizational success, but if leaders don't realize what their people really need to stay motivated, they are missing an opportunity to deliver better results.

Through his research, David Ulrich, a leading management consultant and academic, has found that people find meaning when they see a clear connection between what they value highly and what they spend time doing.[178] When we state a clear sense of purpose for our organization, it draws people towards it for whom that purpose is important. It creates a greater sense of energy and passion to succeed. The work you do matters more.

With a 'sense of purpose' said to be the second most important criterion for millennials considering a job (after salary),[179] purpose is now a differentiator for the best employers.

According to Simon Sinek, author of *Start with Why*,[180] every leader and company knows the 'what'. They can describe their products, their industry and their competitors. Some companies also know the 'how': how they deliver what they need to. Yet few know or articulate their 'why', their purpose, their cause or their belief. The 'why' is their reason for being. And the 'why' is why anyone should care.

How to Get Conscious about Purpose

1. Figure out the 'why' – whether it be at a team or organizational level, drill down in to why you do what you do, and what the driving force behind the work that people need to deliver. If at first you can't grasp the 'why', keep on asking yourself questions to get to the bottom of it.
2. Craft work around purpose – encourage employees to design their work and goals around the core purpose of the organization. This can lead to greater job satisfaction, engagement and resilience.[181]
3. Recognize contribution towards the purpose – employees who are regularly recognized for their contribution experience a greater sense of meaning. Create a culture that talks about and celebrates the positive difference people are making, no matter how small.[182]

Leadership Myths

1. People know what the organization does. They don't need a higher purpose.
2. As long as people are well paid they are happy.

Get Conscious

Do you know what the purpose of the organization is? Is it embedded in the everyday culture? Does everyone who has a relationship with the organization (internal and external) understand the purpose? Do they all contribute to it? Do employees know how they can contribute to the purpose? Are you keeping people connected to the purpose? How do people know that progress is being made towards the organizational purpose?

LESSON 44

Long-term Aims over Short-term Gains

Purpose tends to be a longer-term aim. Yet how do you achieve longer-term ambitions while making money in the short term? Many organizations face this exact challenge. Either a business is trying to make more money or organizations are trying to save it.

But what is the tipping point? At what point does money, and our need for it, get in the way of leaders making good decisions? How does it affect longer-term decision-making? And how committed to our purpose can we be when we simply need to make money? I'm sure there's many a salesperson out there who would turn a blind eye to purpose if it meant landing their next deal. Especially if their bonus depended on it.

Traditionally, companies focused on maximizing shareholder value. Jack Welch, of General Electric fame, was a big proponent of driving shareholder value, and he achieved great success. Yet he changed his mind. He more recently referred to a focus on shareholder value as "the dumbest idea ever".[183] Explaining that we should see shareholder value as the result, not a strategy, with employees, customers and products as the main constituents to focus on.

According to two Harvard Business School professors, Joseph Bower and Lynn Paine, maximizing shareholder value is the error at the heart of corporate leadership and is damaging in practice.[184]

Yet it would be naïve to think that if we were all to turn around and focus on purpose rather than profit that it would automatically lead to success. Purpose and profit can go hand in hand. That's because:

- Generating long-term value for shareholders is good
- Making money is necessary to survive
- Money shouldn't be wasted
- Profit is a reasonable way to measure shareholder value[185]

It's not really a case of whether profit is important or not; most of us would agree that making money is important for a number of reasons. It's more about the 'how you make it' that matters. Simon Sinek says profit isn't a purpose. It's a result. To have purpose means "the things we do are of real value to others".[186] When we focus only on profit, we become short-sighted and often don't think about the long-term ramifications of our actions. Thinking in this way means businesses are at risk of losing the employees and customers who ultimately have the final say over an organization's success. They may not vote with their feet immediately, but if a better offer comes up, they will take their loyalty and custom elsewhere. Shareholders won't be happy either. The fact is, companies that are able to harness the power of purpose to drive performance and profitability enjoy a distinct competitive advantage.[187]

Most organizations that have no overriding purpose other than profit suffer from short-termism. When the imperative is to hit financial targets, decisions become geared around what people can do to make more money. This leads to behaviours that are detached from the needs of the employee and the customer. The numerous examples include banks selling payment protection insurance to customers who do not need it, leaders giving low salaries to employees who can't afford to live, and offering zero hour contracts to provide optimum levels of flexibility to the organization and little security for employees. A myopic focus on profit can strip people of their chance for a more meaningful job, whereas purposeful companies stay focused on long-term performance, even when times are difficult, and are less likely to get distracted by short-term demands.

If employees sense that their organization is only fuelled by profit, their performance and wellbeing can be affected.[188] This is an important consideration as organizations battle for talent and improved retention. It means leaders needing to rethink their purpose, to make sure it meets the needs of everyone involved in making the organization a success.[189]

How to Make Sure Profit Doesn't Run Your Business

1. Think about what you measure – if your systems, reporting and reward mechanisms look largely at financial metrics, you will be driving short-term behaviour that does the same. Consider a balance of hard, target-driven measures as well as behavioural measures. Just because you say that you measure more than money, unless your systems reflect this, it's not true.

2. When times are tough – don't knee jerk into making short-term financial decisions. Stick to the purpose, and your people are more likely to fight harder to get the organization through the difficulties.

3. Look at the services your organization offers – do these reflect your purpose? How do your services uphold your purpose? How do they compromise it? Once you've done a review, consider the services that you may discontinue, and those you might grow in order to drive you closer towards your purpose.

Leadership Myths

1. We need to focus on profit to be successful.
2. Shareholders should be the primary consideration.

Get Conscious

Do you report on more than financial success? If things are 'tight', do you remove activities or investment that supports employees or customers in order to bolster profits? Do you use finances as the main decision-making variable? In the language you use, does finance feature more than any other topic? Are there bad behaviours in the business that are caused by a financial focus? Is remuneration only tied to financial success?

LESSON 45

The Importance of Values

Purpose is just part of the fix, though. Values are important too because unless people know how to behave in an organization, it is less likely that they will be performing 'on purpose'.

Research going back to the 1960s has found there are two sets of employee work behaviours that predict long-term organizational survival and effectiveness:

1. Task performance – the level of effectiveness that an employee has in any particular job or role.
2. Organizational citizenship behaviours – the actions and behaviours of employees that help organizations function more effectively and encourage greater levels of motivation and engagement.

A clear set of organizational values (ways of working, a charter, whatever you wish to call it) helps to guide a more positive and constructive organizational climate.[190] Values get organizations closer to their purpose by establishing procedures that encourage shared views and standards. When striving for excellence, people need guidance around the 'how' behind their 'what' (their day-to-day role). Values still allow people to be themselves, but they create a way of working that everyone can commit to. They set the tone from the start of an individual's relationship with an organization and, as every organizations character will be different, they provide an easy way to get to grips with culture – and fit in. When we fit, we feel better.

Research by Great Place to Work® shows that a strong values-driven culture is critical to the success of high-performing companies that are more likely to have better financial results. Values are related to what we hold close to our hearts, and when there is a disconnect between the value of an individual and that of the organization, it can damage the relationship, because it affects the behaviours and attitudes that define how we treat others every day. The same is true where our values are connected to those of an organization. I've done many interviews where the values of the company have been part of the reason the candidate has turned up in the first place. They can be powerful indicators of an organization's culture and are often the 'emotional' reason that people engage with a new employer.

It's not simply a case of publishing a series of words or statements, though. According to research by Rungway, more than a quarter of employees feel their organization's vision or values have too much corporate jargon, and almost one in five say they don't reflect the company's nature.[191]

Values have to be a true reflection of the culture or if they are aspiration, there needs to be a plan in place to take everyone on a journey to achieving them. Values should become a part of everyday language, a part of everyday life. And when they do, they can play a significant part in delivering purpose and in helping the workforce support each other in achieving it.

How to Bring Values to Life

1. Develop values that matter – capture values that aim to drive the right behaviour. Don't rush the process. Involve the team and ask for suggestions, then hone the values until they are a true reflection of the behaviour you want to see around the organization.

2. Share them – make values visible every day and don't hide them away in a handbook. Refer to them in as many settings as possible, and demonstrate how people are

bringing them to life and supporting progress. Share them with clients and customers, too, through marketing and the way you run the organization – both internally and externally.
3. Revisit them – regularly, to check whether they are still relevant. If they are fine, great; if they aren't, question why.

Leadership Myths
1. Putting values in the handbook is enough to influence behaviour.
2. Values are a waste of time.

Get Conscious
Do you have organizational values? Does anyone know what they are? Do they properly reflect the behaviour of the organization? Do they support the purpose? What do you do to recognize when someone is behaving in a way that makes a positive difference? How could you embed values in your day-to-day processes?

LESSON 46

There's No Purpose Without a Plan

So you have your purpose and a set of values to support the right behaviour. You might even have a mission statement to explain what you intend to do. However, without an actionable plan in place, these things are simply aspirations. This is often where organizations fall down. They create the purpose, they set out the values, but they have no plan, no priorities or organizational goals, to bring the purpose to life. They expect that by creating the lofty vision of what the organization wants to achieve and getting it printed in the handbook and popped on a few wall stickers, that it will materialize. It may get hearts and minds mobilzed if it's communicated well and with passion, but will and enthusiasm don't always lead to action and where they do, they may not be the best action. That's where a plan comes in. And a plan in itself won't achieve what it could with a purpose and values sitting behind it. They support each other and form the foundations for the people delivering the best work.

Especially where there are large groups of people involved. A lack of a plan may work better in a small and agile team who are constantly talking about 'what next' but the larger the organization or team gets, the more intentional you need to become about what needs to be achieved. Research shows that by aligning their efforts, companies can grow up to 58% faster and are 72% more profitable – with strategy forming a clear part of what leads to alignment.[192]

A good strategy helps organizations make good investment decisions and helps to establish priorities so that people know what they are doing and in what order.

Good planning also minimizes the risk of overloading people and duplicated work. And a well-developed strategic plan informs what happens across the entire organization. It informs what the troops focus on and it enables everyone to play a part in delivering the purpose.

How to Build a Strategic Plan

1. Agree on the outcomes – work with the team to figure out what steps you're trying to achieve in pursuit of the purpose. What are the expected results of your efforts?
2. Figure out the KPIs – what are the key measures that matter? Remember that it should be more than money. The money matters (if you deal with money) but also think about clients, people and the other important aspects of delivery.
3. Agree on objectives – what activities will support where you're trying to get to and what is their priority?

Leadership Myths

1. Things change, there is no point in having a plan.
2. People can figure out what the priorities are without clear direction.

Get Conscious

Do you spend your time firefighting? Do you have a clear idea of the priorities, and what needs to be done when? Do you have a plan in place – if not, what is stopping you from creating one? Do you share the plan so others can decide how they can help?

LESSON 47

Goals Keep Us Focused

Everyone in the organization wants to know that they are delivering what is important for success. When leaders are clear about what is important and share that with everyone in the organization, it means that individual goals can be set with clear purpose. Keeping focused at work can be tough, and even with the best of intentions it's easy to get distracted. Often having set our goals for the year, we realize that we've made little or no progress towards them. That's because when organizations set goals, they are often following the traditional process: once a year, as part of the annual appraisal.

Setting effective performance expectations is one of the most significant drivers of performance in organizations. Employees' performance is much better when they are clear about what they are supposed to do and why, and the standards that they'll be measured against.[193] This is why organizational goals have been filtered down for time immemorial in order to keep employees focused on what matters. Yet for years it hasn't worked well. That's because the system has been too inflexible.

Agile goals, which are regularly reviewed and adapted to respond to changing needs, are a great way of connecting people with an organization's purpose while keeping things fluid. Aligning goals in this way gives employees direct influence over the success of their organization and therefore a greater sense of meaning. Individual goals are most effective when they are:
- few in number (three-five)
- focused on the near term (normally around three months)
- aligned to individual strengths

- linked to the organization or team goals so there is a clear 'why'
- set and reviewed regularly to ensure they are still aligned

The difference between a goal and an activity is that an activity is a task that can be guaranteed (in most cases), and a goal is an ambition – it's subject to influence and change. Using football as an example: kicking the ball would be the activity and scoring would be the goal.

Just giving goals to an employee to achieve is less effective. Employees are far more likely to be motivated to deliver a goal when they work in partnership with leaders (see Lesson 1: Work in Partnership with People) to set them. That is because we tend to be more motivated by external evaluation than by our own self-evaluation.[194] And the act of pursuing goals, rather than their achievement, leads to better wellbeing too as we're motivated by making progress – often more so than completing the goal. That's why setting clear and specific goals that we can measure progress against rather than do-your-best instructions tend to be more motivating and achieve better outcomes.[195] It's because making progress towards goals generates dopamine in our brains, which makes us feel good. Dopamine helps us to be focused and keep a positive state of mind.

In goal-setting, the SMART acronym (Specific, Measurable, Attainable, Realistic and Timebound) has been used over the years, but it's outdated and unnecessarily complex. It also doesn't help people set good goals, with many employees believing that their goals are not clear enough.[196]

Clear Review, a performance management software company, has developed a much simpler goal-setting method. They suggest asking these questions when setting goals.

1. **Impact**
   - What are the few things that you can focus on in the near term that will have the greatest impact?
   - What will make the biggest difference right now?
   - Where a longer-term goal needs to be fulfilled, what aspect/s can be completed in the near term?

Impact focuses thinking and helps people prioritize work that will make the biggest difference. While it's important to agree on goals that will impact the team and the organization, effective goals should also take into account the impact on the individual, and what their development needs, aspirations and strengths are. In other words, how the goal will have a personal and positive impact on them. After discussing the impacts, you can look at success factors.

2. **Success Factors**
   - What does success look like?
   - What will the outcomes be if the goal if successfully completed?

The more specific a goal is, the more likely it is that an employee will achieve it, and by detailing success factors, it makes it clearer what a successful outcome would be. There is often where goals fall down – there isn't enough focus on outcomes and it's often too much bout activities. OKRs (Objectives and Key Results) methodology is based on this same philosophy, with 'key results' equating to 'success factors'.

Breaking longer-term goals down in to near-term, specific success factors or key results, and tracking progress, means that goals are more likely to be achieved. Goals in organizations are starting to evolve. They are becoming more transparent with some organizations starting to use collaborative goals to create a more open and collegiate approach to goal setting and achievement.

People should be encouraged to set goals outside of work, too. Having non-work-related goals help us to perform better in all aspects of life, leading to greater wellbeing.[197]

How to Use Goals Effectively

1. Practise – goal-setting is a skill that needs to be developed.
2. Create nudges – we are more likely to stay focused when we are 'nudged' in the right direction. Performance management software that sends alerts can really help, as can putting regular check-ins in the diary to discuss progress.
3. Recognize progress – not only is this motivating, but when people know why something they did was good, they know to repeat it (see Lesson 36: Feedback as a Normal Everyday Act).

Leadership Myths

1. Goals don't ever get done.
2. When reviewing goals, it's best to focus on what hasn't been achieved.

Get Conscious

How focused is your performance? Are you making progress? How do you make sure you focus your efforts in the right way? Do you break goals down into smaller chunks and review your progress? Do you regularly review goals with others and give feedback when you see them making progress?

LESSON 48

Human Policies for Human Beings

The culture an organization wants to create can not only be seen in its purpose and values but in policies too. Yet often, we end up creating policies that only seek to undermine the efforts we're making to create a great culture. This is because policies are often written around worst case scenarios that are there to protect the employer, I call them 'lowest common denominator policies'. It can lead to a lack of flexibility, bureaucratic form-filling and unnecessary approvals. It can also lead to policies which are not very 'grown up'.

This is rarely the intention, of course. Many policies were created to make sure people didn't get unfairly treated or lose out. Yet when we remove any flexibility to deal with individual needs at a team level, and when we remove any flexibility, taking decisions out of the hands of individuals, we end up with policies that are not fit for human purpose and that often don't achieve the right outcomes. An example of this would be an organization that wants to be a flexible employer but has a policy that makes requesting flexibility hard work.

Robotic workplaces are created when the purpose of a policy and what you want it to help achieve are not clearly defined from the outset. How you want it to contribute to the culture and purpose of the organization. What you want it to enable people to do. It can also lead to people 'playing the system': people saying they're sick when they want to go to their child's' nativity play, for example. Or when they arrive and leave on the dot, and take exactly an hour for lunch, because they have been picked up for being late even though they've worked late the night before.

This is a direct result of the way that 'the management' is applying the rules, and results in employees rebelling and not contributing to the organization in the expected way.

It can all be a bit overwhelming for new starters, too. HR spends a lot of time making sure people who join have everything they need. They send out policies, forms, booklets and handbooks, and contracts that you often need a legal degree to fathom. This can detract from the initial experience an individual has had with the leaders and team members they've met. The thing is, an organization's purpose and values need to match their policies. They need to come from the same voice and support the same intentions.

Those intentions need to treat employees as adults and create an environment in which they can take care of their own needs, as well as those of the organization. If we want to run grown-up organizations filled with adults who take responsibility for their own actions, we need to rethink how we make policies, creating them with human needs in mind, which very often means trusting employees to do the right thing.

How to Create Purpose-driven Policies

1. Stop playing to the lowest common denominator – rather than thinking about how the policies could be abused, know that you can trust your people to do the right thing and to make the right decisions.
2. Focus on outcomes – this will make you less concerned about how people are spending every minute of every day. When people know what they have to deliver and when it needs to be done, they take the responsibility to figure out when and how they do it.
3. Remove the formality – assess what needs to be a policy and what can be a 'how to', or part of a set of values or

principles to support the organization's purpose. Then rework your policies so that they are human, easy to read, and reflect a positive and supportive culture rather than a punitive one.

Leadership Myths

1. People want detailed policies to know where they stand.
2. Policies mean people are less likely to break the rules.

Get Conscious

Do your policies play to the lowest common denominator? Do they suggest you trust your people? Do you allow people flexibility to make decisions to meet their own unique needs? Do you take a formal route too early? Are you encouraging grown-up conversations or depending on policies? Are policies getting in the way of good leadership? Are people regularly stepping outside of policy? Why is this? Do your policies reflect who you say you are as an organization?

LESSON 49

Sometimes You Lose Your Way

No matter how purpose driven we are, sometimes we get stuck. Your life can be going along happily, and then you suddenly realize that something is missing - you question the meaning of your life. Or you question whether what you do matters enough. Whether you're making a big enough difference. A life event can trigger it, something seismic that shifts your life, like having children or the death of a loved one. It might be a disconnect between your values and those of the organization, or the fact that you're not being recognized for the contribution you make.

Working environments that support values and purpose support wellbeing. But when the working environment is not supportive in this way, we can struggle to perform.[198]

If we stay stuck in these situations, it can gnaw away at us and make us miserable, disengaged, apathetic and resentful. And many people often feel as though they are stuck. Whether it be a change in our perspective that's needed, whether we need to be honest with how we're feeling, or whether we go elsewhere, we can change our circumstances. Especially if they're significantly affecting how we feel. The starting point is to recognize that there is something to change, and then to recognize that we have the power to change it.

Three common reasons that can lead to people getting 'stuck' are:

1. Lack of honesty – with themselves about how they are really feeling. There is a low-level anxiety getting in the way of them feeling at their best or doing their best work, but they haven't yet admitted it to themselves.

2. Perceived lack of control – this is the most common. Where an individual isn't happy in their role or with their situation, but they don't think they can do anything about it. What's interesting is that often a simple conversation or a few changes to the way that you work, can make all of the difference.

3. We're scared – when we confront our feelings about an issue, it often means having to change our circumstances. Yet many of us don't have the confidence, self-belief or growth mindset to make the change. We often don't feel we have the energy.

What you will find is that when we're held back, when there are barriers in the way of us doing our best at work, or when our work life is negatively affecting our personal life, it requires action. A coach or someone you feel safe speaking to can often help you find your way out of these tricky situations. The one thing to note is that if you stay 'stuck', it can affect your health and wellbeing in the long term and that's no good for you, your performance or the people around you.

How to Get Unstuck

1. Lean in to the 'incongruence' – notice that you're feeling unfilled and think about why that may be. Reflect on whether the current dynamics of your life are giving you the meaning and satisfaction you need and if not, recognize that you can do something about it.

2. Reflect on what makes you happy – what would you be doing if you were not in your current role? Could you do that instead? If not, what part of it could you integrate in to your life? Assess the options and think about what is possible.

3. Focus your energies – once you know what will bring you greater meaning and satisfaction, consider how you are going to make it happen. It may require small or big changes; the key is to focus your attention on bringing this new reality to life, even if it takes time.

Leadership Myths
1. It's hard for me to change my situation.
2. I don't need to be happy at work to be happy.

Get Conscious
Are you happy? Do you feel fulfilled? If you had a year to live, what would you do differently? Are you working towards that now? How much in your life do you do for you? Is there a gap between your values and the values of the environment you're operating in? What's the gap? What's stopping you from making a change? What would need to happen to make you feel happier? What part of that can you make happen?

LESSON 50

Leaders Need Courage

In order to create a compelling purpose, leaders need courage and strength. However, in a work setting, leaders can lack this. Against a backdrop of internal politics, blame, conflict, and performance connected to pay or other remuneration, there can be many obstacles to becoming a brave leader. Even in the most positive organizational climates, knowing that you're making the right decisions, and delivering on purpose, can be challenging.

When leaders are brave, they stand up for their ideas and the ideas of others, they tackle uncomfortable issues, they aren't afraid to try something new, they stand up to bad behaviour and unethical practices, and they know why they are doing these things – they are on purpose.

In contrast, leaders who struggle in this area can fail to influence others and their ideas, can sweep problems under the carpet and can make short-term decisions to achieve short-term success. They can also fail to establish strong and long-lasting relationships as they struggle to establish credibility.

A fixed mindset doesn't help. When leaders fear failure or looking stupid, or when they want to be liked, or when they want to protect their income, they shy away from situations that require courage (see Lesson 34: Effective Leaders Have a Growth Mindset). Very often leaders can sacrifice their own professional values and beliefs to the bureaucracy of the organization. Leaders can stay in denial in order to progress or maintain their position. This can be a consequence of being in an 'over-managed' organization. In effect, these are professional bureaucracies demanding compliance in exchange for progression. So, leaders focus on their work, while maintaining the pretence of professional autonomy.[199] This can impact their sense of meaning and their wellbeing. It will almost certainly affect their performance, as they won't have the freedom of movement needed to try new things or to make decisions that could lead to greater success.

Sometimes leaders don't provide the sponsorship and support that their people need either, and this results in low fulfilment. In an environment where the leaders are too scared, worried, or lacking in confidence to support and champion the ideas and views of others or to commit to a certain direction, performance can be quashed, and employees can feel let down. This affects engagement, performance and wellbeing – because it also affects trust.

Being brave and having courage means being vulnerable. In her book *Dare to Lead*, Brené Brown talks about how leaders need to 'rumble with vulnerability' and face tough situations filled with uncertainty, risk and emotional exposure. Brené's research shows that although fear can derail us, it's actually our ability to get back up when ideas haven't been well received or when something has gone wrong that matters more – this is where courage comes in. She believes in cultivating a culture in which brave work, tough conversations and whole hearts are the expectation, and 'armour' is not necessary or rewarded.[200]

Durable moral courage is "the capacity to persist with morally courageous behaviour even when the initial act elicits rejection, resistance and/or retaliation from within one's organization".[201]

In cultures that support moral courage, leaders are more likely to persist rather than become demoralized by being challenged. This is why brave leaders are so important in delivering purpose.

How to Be a Courageous Leader

1. Champion other people's ideas - when you see a good idea or where one of the team wants to make an improvement, get behind them. Get curious about their plans, help them by building on their ideas, and if approval is needed, support them to get their idea over the finish line.

2. Stand up for what you believe in - this isn't about fighting with people. It's about following through with your ideas and having faith in yourself. It's about lobbying people to support you, despite initial rejection or criticisms. This doesn't mean plowing through regardless of whether your idea is good or not but showing some tenacity and belief in what you're proposing.

3. Stand up to colleagues - when you see other leaders operating in an unhelpful way, speak to them about it. It's not about blaming or punishing them, it's about working together to create the best working environment for everyone. Sometimes you have to put your neck on the line for the greater good. It's partly how you get respect as a leader.

Leadership Myths

1. You can be courageous without being vulnerable.
2. If people think it's a bad idea, there is no point in pushing it.

Get Conscious

Do you stand up for what you believe in? Do you quickly recover when your ideas are knocked back? Do you persist with them? Are you willing to stand up for ideas that may fail? How does it make you feel when you're in conflict with someone over an issue you believe in? Do you presume it's a bad idea because people disagree with you? Does your team believe you are courageous? Why is that

CASE STUDY

Setting Standards
with Actualize Consulting

Situation
Actualize Consulting is a professional services firm that specialize in business process engineering and technology implementations for financial institutions. They needed to find the courage to make significant changes to the way the company operated and how the leadership team behaved.

Challenge
The change was driven by an increasing level of employee turnover, and they decided that something needed to be done when turnover reached 33%. They were spending too much time and money on recruiting and re-recruiting people, and it was having a significant impact on productivity and team morale.

Solution
Actualize decided to transform their culture with a 'Culture Infusion' strategy that identified nine core principles they would use to run the organization. They recognized that the main reason people were leaving was due to strife among the management team on how to run the business, which was trickling down to the teams. Seeing how management led the way in establishing the vibe of the organization, Actualize agreed to work on the management

issues and create an exceptional culture by following these guidelines:

1. Provide intentional leadership – The leadership team worked on building their own self-awareness and got to know people around the business better. They made a focused effort to better understand the aspirations and strengths of everyone on the team.

2. Prioritize personal wellness – Recognizing the importance of emotional and physical energy, they prioritized wellbeing by integrating work/life balance into their organizational culture. The leadership team acted as role models, focusing on their personal wellbeing, and took time off to go to their child's school play, use their lunch break to move around, practise breathing exercises while handling challenging situations and interact in playful ways.

3. Insist on a healthy work/life balance – Everyone was encouraged to achieve a better balance using five simple guiding values of 'breathe', 'move', 'play', 'nourish' and 'replenish' in their day-to-day activities.

4. Practise effective communication – They thought more consciously about the language they used to explain what was important. For instance, a term they adopted was 'time spinning', encouraging people to 'expand' time by slowing down, taking mind breaks, stretching and going for a walk.

5. Handle conflict directly, openly and immediately – in their efforts to handle conflict differently, they promoted the need to be open about feelings. They used their 3P method – Pause to Pivot to a Positive – to change the conversations people were having. Pause by taking a breath and listening to each other. Pivot by trying to think of things from a third-person point of view. And create new positive possibilities by exploring how to move forward together towards a shared resolution.

6. Focus on your people – Every meeting or communication started with a gratitude or a success story.

They enhanced their wellness program and included wellness perks as a significant part of their benefits package.

7. Regularly conduct employee surveys – They started listening to people more, conducting regular surveys and responding to the feedback. For instance, in response to a low score on transparency, they discussed it with their teams and collected ideas on how to improve in that area. It triggered improvements in engagement and transparency led by the leadership team.

8. Align performance rewards with goals – To get everyone aligned with the same vision and to enable employees to deliver against it, they aligned individual goals with the goals of the firm and regularly reviewed progress. Everyone started to use their goals as a working document of their progress throughout the year, like a personal status report.

9. Encourage team connection – By creating more opportunities to connect and encouraging teams to playfully interact inside and outside of work, they reduced stress and built closer relationships, which in turn promoted better teamwork.

Outcome

Since 2016 to the time of writing, the company's employee turnover rate has gone down to 1% from 33% in 2010. Employee performance has been high across all areas of the firm, and employee engagement rates have gone up. The leadership team is now more effective as they operate with one single vision. As the organization has grown, they have made sure they maintain the firm's culture by implementing all the nine principles as the core of their company's operation. The 3P Method is a standardized method of communication all employees are introduced to, and surveys, social activities, wellness challenges and goal alignment keep connections and communication transparent.

CASE STUDY

Getting Passionate
with Brewdog

Situation

Brewdog was started by two brothers in a small town in Scotland in 2007. They wanted to revolutionize the beer industry and make other people as passionate about great craft beer as they were. In their first decade, they opened 46 bars around the globe, and three breweries, and in 2017 they were valued at over £1 billion. They have grown their workforce to over 2,000 and are one of the *Times* Top 100 Best Employers.

Challenge

Brewdog prides itself on having a high-performance culture and is "uncompromising and relentless in their efforts". They take their products and customers seriously, and its employees are 'the crew', without which they wouldn't be where they are today. They want to create the best place to work in the industry and describe their creative and people-centred approach as a "new blueprint for 21st century business".

Solution

Here are just some of the ways they are doing it:
1. The Charter – their daily 'punk' mission guides everything they do: "We bleed craft beer; we are uncompromising; we blow shit up; we are geeks; without us we are nothing."

2. Recruitment based on culture first – hiring from the 1% of people who believe in the Brewdog vision and values. They are 'in this together', so they involve the wider teams in recruitment decisions because they trust everyone to make decisions that will benefit the entire business.
3. Immersing everyone in what they do – with everyone being a Certified Beer Server, with access to sensory training and beer schools.
4. Giving away 20% of their profits – with 10% shared between employees and 10% donated to charity annually through their Unicorn Fund.
5. Giving customers a shareholding – through their Equity for Punks scheme with 70,000 shareholders worldwide.
6. Offering different benefits – contributing between 6% and 10% to everyone's pension, and giving everyone private health care and counselling without referral. As one of the first living wage employers, they update their pay rates every year and even provide 'puppy leave' for new dog owners and a monthly beer allowance.
7. Their open-book policy – keeps everyone updated on key business decisions and changes. They produce weekly production and retail updates, company newsletters, and a publication called *DogTales* where employees can officially put forward business ideas and proposals. The P&L is published monthly too.

Outcome

Brewdog continues to grow at pace and by 2020, they intend to open breweries in China and Australia and more BrewPubs all over the world, and to maintain their fun and fast-paced culture. Crew member wellbeing is essential to Brewdog, as without the team, they have nothing. This is why wellbeing sits as a strategic imperative for the company moving forward.

PURPOSEFUL

A Little Recap

It's the involvement and engagement of everyone involved that helps purposeful organizations achieve their success, but they can only unite and align efforts when people understand what they are heading towards and what behaviours will lead to excellence. Organizations that are only focused on profit miss the opportunity to galvanize the energy of people who want greater meaning in their work.

1. We need to know that our efforts are contributing to something, and that we are making a difference This **search for meaning** enables us to achieve greater fulfilment and when we don't feel appreciated, or when our values are out of kilter with the organization, it can have a negative impact on our performance and wellbeing.
2. Focusing on profit alone can lead to short-terms gains, and missed opportunities for achieving more sustainable and longer-term goals and success. Leaders who **stay focused on longer-term aims** are more likely to make decisions that motivate people to achieve more.
3. **Values show us how we need to behave to achieve organizational** purpose. Through establishing a clear set of expectations that influences everyone's behaviour, organizations are more likely to deliver through an aligned and consistent approach.
4. Establishing purpose is the start of the journey, but without a clear **plan for delivery**, purpose is at risk of not being delivered.
5. When we **set agile goals** that support the purpose, it enables people to focus their efforts in the right way

and find greater meaning as they work towards achieving outcomes that directly support the success of
the organization.

6. We can have an inspiring purpose that guides our path
but without **policies that recognize the needs of people**,
purpose can be compromised. Fair doesn't always mean
treating everyone in the same way, because when we do
this, we can end up playing the system or playing to the
lowest common denominator.

7. **Sometimes we may lose our way** and we struggle to
find the meaning in what we do. We can find greater
meaning through being honest with ourselves and others about what we need.

8. Unless **leaders have courage**, they are unlikely to be
able to deliver on the purpose of the organization nor
stand up for the ideas of others. Yet this bravery is essential to organizational success.

A NOTE TO LEADERS

Creating Well Workplaces
by Paula Leach

> Paula Leach is Former Chief People Officer for The Home Office, now Chief People Officer for the growing global digital resourcing business FDM.

Paula is an inspiring HR professional that I have the privilege to know. Paula is a great role model, not only for women, but for leaders. She has an almost effortless ability to focus on what matters (and was actually the person who finally got me focused on writing this book). With a background in both the private and public sectors, Paula recognizes that for employers to be successful and productive in the future, they will have to get to grips with wellbeing. Here are her thoughts.

Why is Wellbeing So Important for the Future of the Workplace?

We want our workplaces to be optimised for success. If we were to think of each individual human being as a unit of productivity, then we need each unit of productivity to be working to the highest capacity - hence physical and mental attention to the work. We would never be at 100% utilisation, as we need to allow for rest as a key component of optimising utilisation over time - and this is a core tenet of wellbeing.

There is some evidence to suggest that keeping high focus, but for shorter periods and then having longer periods of rest, helps us to work more effectively, and rest should be a factor when designing how any modern workplace operates.

And given that the world is just getting faster and more connected, there is just no way that humans can keep up with that pace. We have tried in the last two decades of technology and globalization to cover the time zones around the world by extending the working day, and we have tried to keep up with technology by answering every email and keeping that scroll bar as small as possible. This is resulting in critical burnout, and we need to change the rules of work. We can't be perfectionists and complete every task anymore. We need to redesign our expectations about the way we work and what we produce. We have to make sure we're prioritizing the high-value elements of our work and that we are setting some non-negotiables when it comes to our own wellbeing.

If we create an environment where people are well and productive, we can layer the critical work on top of that foundation – not the other way around. Otherwise we simply will never get through the priority work, and we will have underutilized individuals and teams who are attending to wellbeing as a consequence, not as a foundation. Wellbeing has to be attended to somewhere. It's better to do this upfront, as the foundation, rather than paying the much higher cost both morally and financially later down the track.

What Will Be the Impact of Digitization and AI?

As you've mentioned in the book, work will be different in the future and not least because of technological advancement, robotization and AI.

Having recently sponsored some research on this, we've found that far from reducing the need for attention to human beings in the future, we will need to increase it. Firstly, if artificial intelligence and robotization take over many of the manual and routine roles that humans perform today, it means that many of the roles that humans play in the workplace, by necessity, will be more complex and likely relational or system-based (connected). So, paying attention to the relational and human aspects of our employees and what they do will come in to greater focus.

Secondly, we can't be convinced that robotization and automation will reduce the need for people in the workplace in the way robotization in manufacturing or logistics has in the past. This is because firstly we will be freeing people up to do more of the complicated/human-only relational work, potentially reducing capacity rather than work. There is an inherent need to understand the human-to-human inter-action, but also the human-to-machine interface, and how that interconnectedness works. Finally, much automation in the future will assist us in dealing with the growing pace, globalization, and data trends that humans can't keep up with in terms of processing.

This means that much of the change will be about ena-bling humans to cope with the pace of the modern world rather than replacing humans. The link to wellbeing is for us to pay attention to how we as humans have our wellbeing needs met and maintain productivity with these changing environments. You talk about conscious intelligence in the book. This will be critical if we want to continue to perform well in the modern world.

What Will the Impact Be on Organizational Design?

There are two main considerations when it comes to organ-izational design and wellbeing. The first relates to the point about technology, because in the future organizations (and Human Resources professionals) will need to understand how to organize the way work gets done and by whom (or by what) in much more depth, with attention paid not only to what humans do but what machines do, and how this flows between human and machine (and customer or service user). Organizational design is also more important in a world where there is increasing pace and complexity (and uncertainty), because it effectively becomes the source of how work gets done, which has a big impact on performance.

Good organizational design also creates clarity and focuses on work that links to clear outcomes. This gives everyone a better view about why their works matters and what is most important. Having a sense of meaning that you've talked about is vital – it does contribute to wellbeing.

What are the Key Aspects to Remember when Developing Our Wellbeing Strategies?

It's important to have clear purpose, as it gives teams and individuals the ability to prioritize effectively and feel more connected to the endeavours of the organization and how their work links to it. It's essentially about creating the WHY of their work and it promotes higher engagement. Any wellbeing strategy should link to that higher purpose and not be a standalone strategy.

Wellbeing strategies should foster a sense of togetherness and feeling part of a community. People need to be able to help, and to be helped and supported. Technology and modern ways of working remotely can really help with this and make sure that even those who work more remotely don't feel socially isolated.

There are many ways that organizations can help to look after the health of people at a more practical level too. From reward and recognition to occupational health schemes, ergonomics, stress management, employee assistance pro-grammes, mental health first aiders – the list nowadays is endless, and these things can make a positive difference. However, while they are really important, they are much less effective if the basic needs of individuals are not met through the relationship between supervisor and employee. If the supervisor or direct manager does not treat individuals in the right way, any wellbeing benefits that you offer to employees are 'sticking plasters'.

Wellbeing strategies need to be mindful of the relationships between line managers and employees, and should work on making those as supportive as possible. This means everything from the way managers speak to individuals (micro behaviours) through to perceived fair treatment such as dealing with performance issues and fair distribution of workload.

It's not just the relationships between managers and employees that are of importance. Relationships in general are fundamental to wellbeing, and there are many experts in the field of neuroscience and behaviour who believe that the Maslow Hierarchy of needs should probably say that the social element is actually the base of the pyramid. We come into the world as babies needing others to survive – at the most basic level we are a collective species for our own survival. Wellbeing strategies need a social angle – helping people to understand themselves and each other better so that they can do great work together.

Flexibility is also important. This might be choice or freedom to move and work in different spaces, to arriving later and having flexible hours. The choice of how work gets done or how a workstation is set up also matter.

Wellbeing should be embedded in the culture, in the way that people behave, what they are focused on and the way that people work. When we get these foundations right and build on that with benefits, we create healthy organizations that can flourish.

CONCLUSION

So, what can we conclude from what we've heard throughout the book?

Wellbeing is about putting back in as much as we're giving out, in order to keep the right balance in our lives. In a world that is becoming increasingly complex and pressurized, and with multiple distractions keeping us from focusing on what matters most, we have to learn a new way of being. A more conscious way of living and leading.

This means becoming conscious of our own needs in order to make decisions and learn what we need to perform and progress. It also means learning more about others and how to support them.

The modern world presents us with endless challenges, and we'll only survive if we do it together. This is why leaders who galvanize people to work together, to support each other and to understand each other will thrive.

Through shared purpose, shared connection and shared understanding, we will create a modern world of work that people cherish and in which people can bring their best selves. Because their best selves matter more than any game face might.

This means getting to know who we really are, what we really want and how to stay our best. Once we figure that out, we can help others to do the same.

The world is going to keep on happening to us, but we don't have to let it break us. If you are prepared to learn, to stay curious, to shelve the ego and to work with others to figure it out, we'll be stronger. We'll learn how to be at our best through becoming more consciously aware.

By becoming more conscious, by holding the mirror up to ourselves and critically assessing who we are and how we are, we can make better decisions about how we lead and how we live. We can make an even more positive difference. We can give ourselves the best chance of a good life. And we will in turn give that 'best chance' to others too.

Now is the era of learning how to be human. How to work better with others. How to inspire each other. How to create shared purpose. How to take better care of the people and the world around us. And how to maintain the energy to forge through and feel good in the process.

It is the era of being conscious. A critical skill for modern day leaders, and the people they lead.

Good luck and welcome to the conscious generation.

ENDNOTES

1   *A Future That Works: Automation, Employment, and Productivity.*
    McKinsey & Company. January 6, 2017.
    https://www.mckinsey.com/~/media/mckinsey/featured%20
    insights/Digital%20Disruption/Harnessing%20automation%20
    for%20a%20future%20that%20works/MGI-A-future-that-
    works-Executive-summary.ashx

2   Call, Kade. "Connected Big Brother: Are We Being Spied
    On Online?" *Business.com.* February 22, 2017.
    https://www.business.com/articles/connected-big-brother-are-
    we-being-spied-on-online/

3   Mire, Michelle. "Why Integrity is the Ultimate Employee Perk."
    Score. February 5, 2018. https://www.score.org/blog/why-integ-
    rity-ultimate-employee-perk

4   Wade, Sophie. "Behind the Rise of Entrepreneurship."
    Fortune. June 12, 2014. http://fortune.com/2014/06/12/
    behind-the-rise-of-entrepreneurship/

5   "Why The Economy is Shifting Towards the Freelance and
    Gig World." *Consultancy.uk.* September 24, 2018.
    https://www.consultancy.uk/news/18759/why-the-economy-is-
    shifting-towards-the-freelance-and-gig-world

6   "5 Negative Effects of High Overtime Levels." *Circadian.*
    December 16, 2018. https://www.circadian.com/blog/item/22-5-
    negative-effects-of-high-overtime-levels.html

7   "Sustaining Employee Engagement & Performance -
    Why Well-being Matters." *Engage for Success.* Published on
    January 27, 2014. https://www.slideshare.net/engage4success/
    e4-s-sustaining-ee-perf-why-well-being-matters

8   Stevenson, Lord Dennis & Farmer, Paul. "Thriving at Work:
    a Review of Mental Health and Employers." Gov.uk.
    October 26, 2017. 5. https://assets.publishing.service.gov.uk/gov-
    ernment/uploads/system/uploads/attachment_data/file/658145/
    thriving-at-work-stevenson-farmer-review.pdf

9   Stevenson, et al., "Thriving at Work: a Review of Mental Health
    and Employers."

10 UK Working Lives. In Search of Job Quality. *CIPD.* 2018. 9.
    https://www.cipd.co.uk/Images/uk-working-lives-summary_
    tcm18-40233.pdf

11 CIPD "UK Working Lives. In Search of Job Quality".

12 *International Comparisons of UK Productivity (ICP)*, Final Estimates: 2016. Office for National Statistics. April 6, 2018. https://www.ons.gov.uk/economy/economicoutputandproductivity/productivitymeasures/bulletins/internationalcomparisonsofproductivityfinalestimates/2016

13 Harter, Jim. *Dismal Employee Engagement Is a Sign of Global Mismanagement*. Gallup. Accessed December 16, 2018. https://www.gallup.com/workplace/231668/dismal-employee-engagement-sign-global-mismanagement.aspx

14 Daly, A.P., Dodge, R., Huyton, J., & Sanders, L.D. "The Challenge of Defining Well-being." *International Journal of Well-being*. August 29, 2012. 230. http://www.internationaljournalof-well-being.org/index.php/ijow/article/viewFile/89/238?origin=publicati

15 "Six-factor Model of Psychological Well-being." *Wikipedia*. Accessed December 16, 2018. https://en.wikipedia.org/wiki/Six-factor_Model_of_Psychological_Well-being

16 *Health and Well-being at Work*. CIPD. May 2018. 2. https://www.cipd.co.uk/Images/health-and-well-being-at-work_tcm18-40863.pdf

17 "Doing Well-being Well." *The Economist Intelligence Unit Limited*. 2018. 4. 5. https://www.adeccogroupfoundation.org/includes/downloads/doing-wellbeing-well.pdf

18 *The Accenture ROI of Well-being Programmes*. ISS. Accessed December 16, 2018. https://betterworkplaces.issworld.com/case/roi-of-well-being-programmes-accenture

19 "How to Measure the ROI on Well-being." *Human Resources Director*. November 9, 2018. https://www.hcamag.com/features/how-to-measure-the-roi-on-well-being-257231.aspx

20 Milligan-Saville, Josie S. et al. "Workplace Mental Health Training for Managers and Its Effect on Sick Leave in Employees: a Cluster Randomised Controlled Trial." *The Lancet*. October 11, 2017. https://www.thelancet.com/journals/lanpsy/article/PIIS2215-0366(17)30372-3/fulltext

21 McGarty, Craig et al. *The Effects of Salient Group Memberships on Persuasion, Small Group Research*. Australian National University. 25 (2). 1994. 267-293. https://www.researchgate.net/publication/247720104_The_Effects_of_Salient_Group_Memberships_on_Persuasion

22 "Leadership." *The English Oxford Living Dictionaries*. Accessed December 18, 2018. https://en.oxforddictionaries.com/thesaurus/leadership

23 "Leadership". *Thesaurus.com*. Accessed December 18, 2018.
https://www.thesaurus.com/browse/leadership

24 Delizonna, Laura. "High-Performing Teams Need Psychological Safety. Here's How to Create It." *Harvard Business Review*.
August 24, 2017. https://hbr.org/2017/08/high-perform-
ing-teams-need-psychological-safety-heres-how-to-create-it

25 Lebowitz, Shana. "Google Considers This to Be the Most Critical
Trait of Successful Teams." *Business Insider*. November 20, 2015.
https://www.businessinsider.com/amy-edmondson-on-psycho-
logical-safety-2015-11?r=UK&IR=T

26 Austin, Tim. "Making It Safe: the Importance of
Psychological Safety." *Safety Differently*. March 9, 2017.
http://www.safetydifferently.com/making-it-safe-the-impor-
tance-of-psychological-safety/

27 Schein, Edgar H. "How Can Organizations Learn Faster?
The Challenge of Entering the Green Room." *Sloan Management
Review*. 1993. 34:85–92. https://sloanreview.mit.edu/article/
how-can-organizations-learn-faster-the-challenge-of-entering-
the-green-room/

28 Kark, Ronit, & Carmeli, Abraham. "Alive and Creating: the
Mediating Role of Vitality and Aliveness in the Relationship
Between Psychological Safety and Creative Work Involvement."
Journal of Organizational Behaviour. 2008. .30(6):785–804 .
https://doi.org/10.1002/job.571

29 Schneider, Gary. *Business Studies Journal*, Volume 3. Quinnipiac
University. 2011. 31. https://www.abacademies.org/articles/
bsjvol312011.pdf

30 Kahn, William A. "Psychological Conditions of Personal Engagement and Disengagement at Work." *Academy of Management
Journal*. 1990. 33:694. http://www.jstor.org/stable/256287

31 Berne, Eric. *Transactional Analysis*. Eric Berne MD. Accessed
December 18, 2018. http://www.ericberne.com/transaction-
al-analysis/

32 "Albert Mehrabian." *Wikipedia*. Last Edited 19 April, 2018.
https://en.wikipedia.org/wiki/Albert_Mehrabian

33 Lunney, J., Lueder, S. & O'Connor, G. "Postmortem Culture:
How You Can Learn from Failure." *re:Work*. April 24, 2018.
https://rework.withgoogle.com/blog/postmortem-culture-how-
you-can-learn-from-failure/

34   Stone, Mark. "What We Can Learn from Elon Musk's Unbalanced Ratio of Failures To Successes". *Forbes*. January 3, 2018. https://www.forbes.com/sites/delltechnologies/2018/01/03/what-we-can-learn-from-elon-musks-unbalanced-ratio-of-failures-to-successes/#1870af9a7374

35   Sims, Peter. "Five of Steve Job's Biggest Mistakes". *Harvard Business Review*. January 21, 2013. https://hbr.org/2013/01/five-of-steve-jobss-biggest-mi

36   Swami, Viren. "Most of Us Tend to be Attracted to People Who are Similar to Ourselves". *PsyPost*. March 28, 2017. https://www.psypost.org/2017/03/us-tend-attracted-people-similar-48596

37   Hunt, V., Layton, D. & Prince, S. *Diversity Matters*. McKinsey and Company. 2015. https://assets.mckinsey.com/~/media/857F440109AA4D13A54D9C496D86ED58.ashx

38   DeWall, Nathan. & Bushman, Brad. "Social Acceptance and Rejection: the Sweet and the Bitter". *Current Directions in Psychological Science*. 2011. 20 (4): 256.10.1177/0963721411417545

39   Mineo, Liz. "Good Genes Are Nice, But Joy Is Better". *The Harvard Gazette*. April 11, 2017. https://news.harvard.edu/gazette/story/2017/04/over-nearly-80-years-harvard-study-has-been-showing-how-to-live-a-healthy-and-happy-life/

40   "Inclusion". *Merriam-Webster*. Last updated December 6, 2018. https://www.merriam-webster.com/dictionary/inclusion

41   Krauss Whitbourne, Susan. "Turn Down Your Brain's Worry Center". *Psychology Today*. October 9, 2012. https://www.psychologytoday.com/gb/blog/fulfillment-any-age/201210/turn-down-your-brain-s-worry-center

42   Fica, Tori. *What People Really Want from Onboarding*. Bamboo HR. October 3, 2018. https://www.bamboohr.com/blog/onboarding-infographic/?utm_source=Par-Bnusly-Ref&utm_medium=referral&utm_campaign=10-surprising-employee-retention-statistics-you-need-to-know-blog

43   *2018 Job Seeker Nation Study*. Jobvite. 2018. https://www.jobvite.com/wp-content/uploads/2018/04/2018_Job_Seeker_Nation_Study.pdf

44   Pogosyan, Marianna. "On Belonging". *Psychology Today*. April 11, 2017. https://www.psychologytoday.com/gb/blog/between-cultures/201704/belonging

45   *Why Employees Need Workplace Flexibility*. The Sloan Center, Boston College. Accessed December 18, 2018. http://workplaceflexibility.bc.edu/need/need_employees

46 A Manifesto For Change – A Modern Workplace For a Flexible Workforce. *Timewise and Deloitte*. 2018. 2. https://timewise. co.uk/wp-content/uploads/2018/05/Manifesto-for-change.pdf

47 *Autonomy in the Workplace Has Positive Effects on Well-being and Job Satisfaction, Study Finds*. University of Birmingham. April 25, 2017. https://www.birmingham.ac.uk/news/latest/2017/04/autonomy-workplace.aspx

48 *The Next 250K*. Leesman. Accessed December 18, 2018. 8. https://www.leesmanindex.com/250k_Report.pdf

49 Ibid

50 Leesman. *The Next 250K*. 18.

51 Channon, Ben. *Happy by Design: a Guide to Architecture and Mental Well-being*. London. Riba Publishing. 2018.

52 "Brief Diversions Vastly Improve Focus, Researchers Find". *Science Daily*. February 8, 2011. https://www.sciencedaily.com/releases/2011/02/110208131529.htm

53 Cooper, Belle Beth. "5 Unusual Ways to Start Working Smarter, Not Harder, Backed By Science". *Buffer*. Last updated April 4, 2016. https://blog.bufferapp.com/5-ways-to-get-more-done-by-working-smarter-not-harder

54 Bradberry, T. & Greaves, J. *Emotional Intelligence 2.0*. San Diego. TalentSmart. 2009.

55 *Mind's Workplace Well-being Index 2017/18*. Mind. 2018. 5. https://www.mind.org.uk/media/25781370/workplace-wellbeing-index-insights-report-2017-18.pdf?ctaId=/workplace/workplace-wellbeing-index/slices/index-201617-insights-report/

56 *Mental Health in the Workplace*. Mental Health Foundation. Accessed December 17, 2018. https://www.mentalhealth.org.uk/our-work/mental-health-workplace

57 *Poor Mental Health Support Costs Employers "Billions" – New Report*. NHS Employers. October 25, 2017. https://www.nhsemployers.org/news/2017/10/poor-mental-health-support-costs-employers-billions-new-report

58 Stevenson, et al."Thriving at Work: a Review of Mental Health and Employers."

59 Stevenson, et al. "Thriving at Work: a Review of Mental Health and Employers."

60 "Worried About Your Mental Health? How to get Treatment and Support – The Signs." *Rethink Mental Illness*. Accessed December 17, 2018. https://www.rethink.org/diagnosis-treatment/symptoms/worried-about-your-mental-health/the-signs?gclid=CjwK-CAiAlb_fBRBHEiwAzMeEdind6xDsDMQUrYfuauSRBpif8A1g-fDHx9CSeot4pgpxKNyLn_8OAihoCRVMQAvD_BwE

61 Vaughan-Jones, Helen & Barham, Leela. *Healthy Work – Evidence into Action*. Bupa. 2010. 46 Figure 9.

62 Hannibal, Kara. E. & Bishop, Mark. D. "Chronic Stress, Cortisol Dysfunction, and Pain: a Psychoneuroendocrine Rationale for Stress Management in Pain Rehabilitation". *Physical Therapy, Oxford Academic*. December 1, 2014. 16 - 18. https://academic.oup.com/ptj/article/94/12/1816/2741907

63 *Healthy Lifestyle Stress Management*. Mayo Clinic. April 21, 2016. https://www.mayoclinic.org/healthy-lifestyle/stress-management/in-depth/stress/art-20046037

64 *Workplace Stress*. The American Institute of Stress. Accessed December 17, 2018. https://www.stress.org/workplace-stress/

65 Pfeffer, Jeffrey. *Dying for a Paycheck*. HarperCollins. New York. 2018. 3, 8.

66 Cachia, Moira & Whitfield, Matthew. *How Does Workplace Stress Affect Job Performance?* University of West London. 2018. https://repository.uwl.ac.uk/id/eprint/4083/1/Whitfield-Cachia-2018-How-does-workplace-stress-affect-job-performance.pdf

67 *Stress and Heart Disease*. The American Institute of Stress. Accessed December 17, 2018. https://www.stress.org/stress-and-heart-disease

68 Cuncic, Arlin. "Amygdala Hijack and the Fight or Flight Response." *Very Well Mind*. October, 26, 2018. https://www.verywellmind.com/what-happens-during-an-amygdala-hijack-4165944

69 Scarlett, Hilary. *Neuroscience for Organizational Change*. London. Kogan. 2016. 25.

70 Scarlett. *"Neuroscience for Organizational Change"*. 38.

71 Rathje, Steve. "The Power of Framing: It's Not What You Say, It's How You Say It." *The Guardian*. July 20, 2017. https://www.theguardian.com/science/head-quarters/2017/jul/20/the-power-of-framing-its-not-what-you-say-its-how-you-say-it

72 *The Importance of Vulnerability*. The School Of Life. September 21, 2017. https://www.youtube.com/watch?v=PJsJ96yyVk8

73 Gander, Kashmira. "Why You Need To Stop Stressing About Being Perfect." *The Independent*. February 3, 2017. https://www.independent.co.uk/life-style/why-stop-stressing-being-perfect-perfectionism-life-coach-happiness-lifestyle-mental-health-a7560131.html

74 The School of Life. *"The Importance of Vulnerability."*

75 Young, Valerie. *The Secret Thoughts of Successful Women*. New York. Crown Business. 2011.

76 Dweck, Carol. *The Power of Believing You Can Improve*. TED. November, 2014. https://www.ted.com/talks/carol_dweck_the_power_of_believing_that_you_can_improve?language=en

77 Langford, Joe & Clance, Pauline Rose. "The Impostor Phenomenon: Recent Research Findings Regarding Dynamics, Personality and Family Patterns and Their Implications for Treatment." *Psychotherapy Theory Research, Practice, Training*. Fal January 1993.

78 Langford, et al. "The Imposter Phenomenon: Recent Research Findings Regarding Dynamics, Personality and Family Patterns and Their Implications."

79 "Good Enough Parent". *Wikipedia*. Last Edited 13 January, 2019. https://en.wikipedia.org/wiki/Good_enough_parent

80 Winnicott, D.W. *The Maturational Process and the Facilitating Environment: Studies in the Theory of Emotional Development*. The Hogarth Press and the Institute of Psycho-Analysis. 1965. http://doctorabedin.org/wp-content/uploads/2015/07/Donald-Winnicott-The-Maturational-Process-and-the-Facilitating-Environment-1965.pdf

81 Slutsky, J., Chin, B., Raye, J. & Creswell, J.D. *Mindfulness Training Improves Employee Well-being: a randomized controlled trial*. J Occup Health Psychol. October 2018. https://www.researchgate.net/publication/327043868_Mindfulness_Training_Improves_Employee_Well-Being_A_Randomized_Controlled_Trial

82 Eby, L.T. et al. "Mindfulness-based Training Interventions for Employees: a Qualitative Review of the Literature". *Human Resource Management Review*. 2017. https://www.researchgate.net/publication/315810543_Mindfulness-based_training_interventions_for_employees_A_qualitative_review_of_the_literature

83 Ireland, Tom. "What Does Mindfulness Meditation Do to Your Brain?" *Scientific American*. June 12, 2014. https://blogs.scientificamerican.com/guest-blog/what-does-mindfulness-meditation-do-to-your-brain/

84 Bradberry, Travis. "5 Ways You Can Use Mindfulness to Fix Your Brain, Reduce Stress and Boost Performance." *Forbes.* April 1, 2016. https://www.forbes.com/sites/travisbradberry/2016/04/01/5-ways-you-can-use-mindfulness-to-fix-your-brain-reduce-stress-and-boost-performance/#77a6a9be2714]

85 *Overview – Dyslexia.* NHS. July 30, 2018. https://www.nhs.uk/conditions/dyslexia/

86 Short, Hannah. "Let's Talk Menopause Because We Are Failing 13 Million Women." *The Guardian.* April 1, 2015. https://www.theguardian.com/healthcare-network/2015/apr/01/lets-talk-menopause-because-we-are-failing-13-million-women

87 *Stress In America: State of Our Nation.* American Psychological Association. November 1, 2017. https://www.apa.org/images/state-nation_tcm7-225609.pdf

88 "Great Britain and Stress – How Bad Is It and Why Is It Happening?" *Forth.* February 4, 2018. https://www.forthwithlife.co.uk/blog/great-britain-and-stress/

89 *Research Report.* CIPD. 2017. https://www.cipd.co.uk/Images/financial-well-being-practical-guidance-report_tcm18-17440.pdf

90 *How Do You Test For Dyslexia?* The Dyslexia Association. 2018. https://www.dyslexia.uk.net/what-is-dyslexia/dyslexia-test

91 CIPD. *"Research Report."*

92 *National Careers Week*. NCW. Accessed December 18, 2018. https://nationalcareersweek.com/

93 Feloni, Richard. "Facebook's Lead HR Consultant Says These Are The 3 Most Common Mistakes New Managers Make." *Business Finder.* May 4, 2016. https://www.businessinsider.com/marcus-buckingham-most-common-management-mistakes-2016-5?r=US&IR=T

94 Butterworth, P., Leach, L.S., Strazdins, L., Olesen, S.C., Rodgers, B. & Broom, D.H. "The Psychosocial Quality of Work Determines Whether Employment Has Benefits for Mental Health: Results from a Longitudinal National Household Panel Survey." *Occupational & Environmental Medicine.* Accessed December 18, 2018. http://dx.doi.org/10.1136/oem.2010.059030

95 Faragher, E.B., Cooper, C.L. & Cass, M. "The Relationship Between Job Satisfaction and Health: a Meta-analysis." *Occupational & Environmental Medicine.* Accessed December 18, 2018. https://oem.bmj.com/content/62/2/105#ref-2

96   Maulabakhsh, Raheela & Raziq, Abdul. "Impact of
     Working Environment on Job Satisfaction." *Science
     Direct.* October 30, 2014. https://ac.els-cdn.com/
     S2212567115005249/1-s2.0-S2212567115005249-main.
     pdf?_tid=1967a0fc-9e53-4b8b-849e-65eb97ccd8ff&acd-
     nat=1541956565_2e9e124c9d65ea81aaddca80946ee19a

97   "The Wheel of Life". *Mind Tools.* Accessed December 18, 2018.
     https://www.mindtools.com/pages/article/newHTE_93.htm

98   "It's Now a Proven Fact - Your Unconscious Mind Is Running
     Your Life!" *Life Trainings.* Accessed December 13, 2018.
     http://www.lifetrainings.com/Your-unconscious-mind-is-run-
     ning-you-life.html

99   *Your unconscious mind is ruining your life,* Life Trainings;
     "It's Now a Proven Fact - Your Unconscious Mind Is Running
     Your Life!" *Life Trainings.* Accessed December 13, 2018.
     http://www.lifetrainings.com/Your-unconscious-mind-is-run-
     ning-you-life.html

100 Jamieson, David W. & Cheung-Judge, Mee-Yan. "Providing
     Deeper Understanding of the Concept of Use of Self in OD
     Practice". OD Practitioner. Vol. 50 No. 4. 2018.
     https://static1.squarespace.com/static/545a8a95e4b09bb-
     f6a28a9e4/t/5bd1a266652dea1600886168/1540465809996/
     Providing+Deeper+Understanding+of+the+con-
     cept+of+the+%27use+of+self%27+in+OD+practice

101 "Johari Window." *Wikipedia.* Accessed December 13, 2018.
     https://en.wikipedia.org/wiki/Johari_window

102 *Leadership and Self-Deception: Getting out of the Box.*
     The Arbinger Institute. San Francisco. Berrett-Koehler. 2000.

103 Zenger, Jack & Folkman, Joseph. "Overcoming Feedback Phobia:
     Take The First Step." *The Harvard Business Review.*
     December 16, 2013. https://hbr.org/2013/12/overcoming-feed-
     back-phobia-take-the-first-step

104 Christy, A.G., Rivera, G.N., Kim, J., Hicks, J.A., Vess, M. &
     Schlegel, R. J. "Understanding the Relationship Between Per-
     ceived Authenticity and Well-being." *Review of General Psychol-
     ogy.* November 15, 2018. http://dx.doi.org/10.1037/gpr0000161

105 Dara Narahan, Betsy. "The Mask of the Personality." *Phoenix
     Tools,* April 1, 2014. https://phoenixtools.org/mask-personality/

106 Ashkanasy, Neal & Fisher, Cynthia. "The Emerging Role of
     Emotions in Work Life: an Introduction." *Journal of Organiza-
     tional Behaviour.* 21: 123–129. 2000. http://citeseerx.ist.psu.edu/
     viewdoc/download?doi=10.1.1.321.44&rep=rep1&type=pdf

107 Hampton, Debbie. "The Neuroscience of Changing Your Behaviour." *The Best Brain Possible.* January 8, 2017. https://www.thebestbrainpossible.com/the-neuroscience-of-changing-your-behaviour/

108 Hani, Julie. "The Neuroscience of Behaviour Change." *Health Transformer.* August 2017. https://healthtransformer.co/the-neuroscience-of-behavior-change-bcb567fa83c1

109 Berkman, Elliot. "The Neuroscience of Goals and Behavioural Change." *Consulting Psychology Journal Practice and Research.* September 2017. https://www.researchgate.net/publication/318542415_The_Neuroscience_of_Goals_and_Behaviour_Change

110 "How We Are Easily, Too Easily, Triggered." *The Book of Life.* Accessed 15 December, 2018. https://www.theschooloflife.com/thebookoflife/how-we-are-easily-triggered-and-why/

111 Bell, Poorna. "Steve Peters, Author Of The Chimp Paradox, Reveals How to Be Less Anxious." *Huffpost.* May 14, 2014. https://www.huffingtonpost.co.uk/2014/05/14/steve-peters-chimp-paradox_n_5321142.html

112 Lyubansky, Mikhail. "Studies of Unconscious Bias: Racism Not Always by Racists." *Psychology Today.* April 26, 2012. https://www.psychologytoday.com/us/blog/between-the-lines/201204/studies-unconscious-bias-racism-not-always-racists

113 Navarro, Renee J. *Unconscious Bias.* Office of Diversity and Outreach. Accessed on December 15, 2018. https://diversity.ucsf.edu/resources/unconscious-bias

114 "Halo Effect." *Wikipedia.* Accessed December 15, 2018. https://en.wikipedia.org/wiki/Halo_effect

115 "Bias." *Psychology Today.* Accessed December 15, 2018. https://www.psychologytoday.com/us/basics/bias

116 Bennie, Maureen. *What is Neurodiversity?* Autism Awareness Centre Inc. April, 12 2016. https://autismawarenesscentre.com/un-adopts-new-goals-disabilities/

117 Valentine, Michael. *Influencing Behaviour During Planned Culture Change: a Participatory Action Research Case Study.* Antioch University. 2016. https://aura.antioch.edu/cgi/viewcontent.cgi?referer=https://www.google.com/&httpsredir=1&article=1330&context=etds

118 Tancock, Christopher. "Why (and How) We Need to Kick the Habit: Exploring Unconscious Bias." *Elsevier.* November 16, 2017. https://www.elsevier.com/connect/editors-update/why-and-how-we-need-to-kick-the-habit-exploring-unconscious-bias

119 "Communication." *English Oxford Living Dictionaries.*
Accessed December 16, 2018. https://en.oxforddictionaries.com/
definition/communication

120 Fisher, Anne. "Employees Would Rather Hear Bad News
Than No News." *Fortune.* February 17, 2016. http://fortune.
com/2016/02/17/employees-transparency-bad-news/

121 Diaz-Uda, A., Medina, C. & Schill, B. "Diversity's New Frontier."
Deloitte Insights. July 23, 2013. https://www2.deloitte.com/
insights/us/en/topics/talent/diversitys-new-frontier.html

122 Chakkol, Mehmet & Johnson, Mark. *Benefits Realization from
Collaborative Working.* Institute for Collaborative Working.
November 2015. https://instituteforcollaborativeworking.com/
Resources/Documents/collaborative_working_benefits_realiza-
tion_report.pdf

123 Grant, A., Gino, F. & Hofmann, D.A. "The Hidden Advantages of
Quiet Bosses." *Harvard Business Review.* December 2010. https://
hbr.org/2010/12/the-hidden-advantages-of-quiet-bosses

124 Duncan, Roger Dean. "The Why of Work: Purpose and Meaning
Really Do Matter." *Forbes.* September 11, 2018. https://www.
forbes.com/sites/rodgerdeanduncan/2018/09/11/the-why-of-
work-purpose-and-meaning-really-do-matter/#33fc750168e1

125 Wright,J., Nadelhoffer, T., Perini, T., Lagville, A., Echols,
M. & Venezia, K. "The Psychological Significance of Humility."
The Journal of Positive Psychology. April 22, 2016.
https://www.researchgate.net/publication/301597661_
The_psychological_significance_of_humility

126 Hammond, M.D., Girme, Y. U., Low, R.S. and Overall, N.C.
"Emotional Suppression During Personal Goal Pursuit Impedes
Goal Strivings and Achievement." *Emotion* Vol 17 (2), (2017)
Washington D.C.

127 Heerdink, M.W., Homan, A.C. & van Kleef, G.A. "Emotional
Influence in Groups: the Dynamic Nexus of Affect, Cognition,
and Behaviour." *Current Opinion in Psychology.* 17, 156-161. 2017.
https://doi.org/10.1016/j.copsyc.2017.07.017

128 Duhigg, Charles. "What Google Learned from Its Quest to
Build the Perfect Team." *The New York Times Magazine.*
February 25, 2016. https://www.nytimes.com/2016/02/28/mag-
azine/what-google-learned-from-its-quest-to-build-the-perfect-
team.html?_r=0

129 "The Nature of Conflict." *Conflict Management.* Accessed
December 16, 2018. http://www.cios.org/encyclopedia/conflict/
Cnature3_destructive.htm

130 Ekman, Paul. *Emotions Revealed: Recognizing Faces and Feelings to Improve Communication and Emotional Life*. New York. Henry Holt. 2007.15.

131 "Denise Rousseau." *Wikipedia*. Last edited November 1, 2017. https://en.wikipedia.org/wiki/Denise_Rousseau

132 Uhereczky, Agnes & Vadkerti, Zoltan. *"10 Global Trends and Their Impact on Fundamental Human Needs."* Human Dynamics and Work Department. July 7, 2015. http://worklifehub.com/assets/files/Herman-Miller-White-paper-2015-WLH.pdf

133 "Drive: the Surprising Truth About What Motivates Us." *Wikipedia*. Last edited November 13, 2018. https://en.wikipedia.org/wiki/Drive:_The_Surprising_Truth_About_What_Motivates_Us

134 "UK L&D Report: 2018: Benchmark Your Workplace Learning Strategy." *Findcourses.co.uk*. 2018. 7. https://www.findcourses.co.uk/file/1627/download

135 Haims, J., Stempel, J. & van der Vyver, B. "Learning and Development. Into the Spotlight." *Deloitte Insights*. February 27, 2015. https://www2.deloitte.com/insights/us/en/focus/human-capital-trends/2015/learning-and-development-human-capital-trends-2015.html

136 Schwantes, Marcel. "Why Are Your Employees Quitting? A Study Says It Comes Down to Any of These 6 Reasons." *Inc.com*. October 23, 2017. https://www.inc.com/marcel-schwantes/why-are-your-employees-quitting-a-study-says-it-comes-down-to-any-of-these-6-reasons.html

137 Bevan, Stephen. *Managing Staff Retention*. Institute for Employment Studies. Accessed December 18, 2018. https://www.employment-studies.co.uk/system/files/resources/files/mp7.pdf

138 Bersin Josh. "Employee Retention Now a Big Issue: Why the Tide Has Turned." *LinkedIn*. August 16, 2013. https://bit.ly/2E5QK9e

139 "How Companies Can Profit from a 'Growth Mindset'." *Harvard Business Review*. November 2014. https://hbr.org/2014/11/how-companies-can-profit-from-a-growth-mindset

140 Dweck, Carol. "What Having a 'Growth Mindset' Actually Means." *Harvard Business Review*. January 13, 2016. https://hbr.org/2016/01/what-having-a-growth-mindset-actually-means%203/4

141 Ibid

142 *Idea Report. Growth Mindset Culture*. Neuroleadership Institute. 2018. https://bit.ly/2Sujj8H

143 "Growth Mindset at Work: How Beliefs About the Nature of Talents and Abilities Shape Organizational Success." *Paradigm*. 2018. 12. http://info.paradigmiq.com/growth_mindset_white_paper

144 Dweck, C., Murphy, M., Chatman, J. & Key, L. *New Study Findings – Why Fostering a Growth Mindset in Organizations Matters.* Senn Delaney. 2014. 2. http://knowledge.senndelaney.com/docs/thought_papers/pdf/stanford_agilitystudy_hart.pdf

145 Cox, C., Grant., H. & Rock, D. "Organizational Growth Mindset." *Neuroleadership Journal.* October 2015.

146 Sorenson, Susan. "How Employees' Strengths Make Your Company Stronger." *Gallup Business Journal.* February 20, 2014. https://news.gallup.com/businessjournal/167462/employees-strengths-company-stronger.aspx

147 Aguinus, H., Gottfredson, R. & Joo, H. *Delivering Effective Performance Feedback: the Strengths-based Approach.* Kelley School of Business. January 2011. https://www.researchgate.net/publication/251550792_Delivering_effective_performance_feedback_The_strengths-based_approach

148 Rigoni, Brandon & Asplund, Jim. "Strengths-based Employee Development: the Business Results." *Gallup Workplace.* July 7, 2016. https://www.gallup.com/workplace/236297/strengths-based-employee-development-business-results.aspx

149 Mueller-Hanson, Rose & Pulakos, Elaine. *Transforming Performance Management to Drive Performance: an Evidence-Based Roadmap.* New York. Routledge. 2018.

150 Mueller-Hanson et al. *"Transforming Performance Management to Drive Performance: an Evidence-Based Roadmap."* 151.

151 Wilkinson, David. "The Oxford Review Research-Based Guide to Unlearning. The Oxford Review Research-Based Guide to Unlearning." *The Oxford Review.* January 2018.

152 Seijts, Gerard. "Good Leaders Never Stop Learning." *Ivey Business Journal.* August 2013. https://iveybusinessjournal.com/publication/good-leaders-never-stop-learning/

153 Staats, Bradley. *Never Stop Learning: Stay Relevant, Reinvent Yourself, and Thrive.* Boston. The Harvard Printed Press. 2018.

154 Duncan, Roger Dean. "Want To Stay Relevant? Never Stop Learning." *Forbes.* June 4, 2018. https://www.forbes.com/sites/rodgerdeanduncan/2018/06/04/want-to-stay-relevant-never-stop-learning/#1b0c01637180

155 Vaccaro, Adam. "The Best Leaders Ask For More Feedback." *Inc. com.* December 24, 2013. https://www.inc.com/adam-vaccaro/best-leaders-ask-for-more-feedback.html

156 Manyika, J., Chui, M., Miremadi, M., Bughin, J., George, K., Willmott, P. & Dewhurst, M. *Harnessing Automation for a Future That Works.* McKinsey Global Institute. January 2017. https://www.mckinsey.com/featured-insights/digital-disruption/harnessing-automation-for-a-future-that-works

157 "Insights From the Flex Office Conference 2018." *Orega.* September 26, 2018. https://blog.orega.com/flex-office-conference-2018-office-evolution-insights.

158 Daugherty, Paul & Williams, Greg. *Highlights – Human & Machine.* Accessed December 17, 2018. https://www.youtube.com/watch?v=S4nhUiR9puY

159 *Good Work: the Taylor Review of Modern Working Practices.* Gov.uk. May 4, 2018. https://assets.publishing.service.gov.uk/government/uploads/system/uploads/attachment_data/file/627671/good-work-taylor-review-modern-working-practices-rg.pdf

160 Daugherty et al. *"Highlights – Human & Machine."*

161 Haughton, Jermaine. *How to Define Your Business Purpose.* Chartered Management Institute. July 24, 2018. https://www.managers.org.uk/insights/news/2018/july/how-to-define-your-business-purpose

162 *People on a Mission.* Korn Ferry Institute. 2016. 2. http://cashmanleadership.com/site/wp-content/uploads/2016/12/Korn-Ferry_People-on-a-mission_Dec2016.pdf

163 *Meaningful Brands.* Havas Media. 2015. https://www.havasmedia.de/media/mb17_brochure_print_ready_final-min.pdf

164 Korn Ferry Institue *"People on a Mission."* 2.

165 *2017 Edelman Trust Barometer.* Edelman. 2017.10. https://www.slideshare.net/EdelmanInsights/2017-edelman-trust-barometer-global-results-71035413

166 *Culture of Purpose – Building Business Confidence; Driving Growth. 2014 Core Beliefs & Culture Survey.* Deloitte. 2014. 11. https://www2.deloitte.com/content/dam/Deloitte/us/Documents/about-deloitte/us-leadership-2014-core-beliefs-culture-survey-040414.pdf

167 *2015 Cone Communications / Ebiquity Global CSR Study.* Cone. 2015. 11, 18. http://www.conecomm.com/2015-cone-communications-ebiquity-global-csr-study-pdf

168 *Putting Purpose to Work: a Study of Purpose in the Workplace."* PWC. June 2016. 5. https://www.pwc.com/us/en/about-us/corporate-responsibility/assets/pwc-putting-purpose-to-work-purpose-survey-report.pdf

169 Ibid

170 Mainwaring, Simon. "Marketing 3.0 Will Be Won by Purpose-driven, Social Brands." *Forbes*. July 16, 2013. https://www.forbes.com/sites/simonmainwaring/2013/07/16/marketing-3-0-will-be-won-by-purpose-driven-social-brands-infographic/#785cedcf1886

171 Collins, Sam. *Finding Your Purpose*. YouTube. June 10, 2018. https://www.youtube.com/watch?v=DLECPc_AbTk

172 *The What, the Why and the How of Purpose*. Chartered Management Institute. Accessed December 18, 2018. https://www.managers.org.uk/Campaigns/Purpose-in-Business

173 *Global Human Capital Trends 2015*. Deloitte University Press. 2015. 11. https://www2.deloitte.com/content/dam/Deloitte/na/Documents/human-capital/na_DUP_GlobalHumanCapital-Trends2015.pdf

174 *Putting Purpose to Work: a Study of Purpose in the Workplace*. PWC. June 2016. 3. https://www.pwc.com/us/en/about-us/corporate-responsibility/assets/pwc-putting-purpose-to-work-purpose-survey-report.pdf

175 Pink, Daniel H. *Drive: the Surprising Truth About What Motivates Us*. New York. Riverhead Books. 2009.

176 Schaefer, S.M., Boylan, J.M., van Reekem, C.M., Lapate, R.C., Norris, C.J., Ryff, C.D. & Davidson, R. J. "Purpose in Life Predicts Better Emotional Recovery from Negative Stimuli." *Plos One*. November 13, 2013. https://journals.plos.org/plosone/article?id=10.1371/journal.pone.0080329

177 PWC. *"Putting Purpose to Work: a Study of Purpose in the Workplace."* 7.

178 Duncan. *"The Why of Work: Purpose and Meaning Really Do Matter."*

179 Hewko, John. *This is What Millennials Want in 2018*. World Economic Forum. January 10, 2018. https://www.weforum.org/agenda/2018/01/this-is-what-millennials-want-in-2018

180 Sinek, Simon. *"Start with Why."* Penguine. 2009.

181 Berg, J.M., Dutton, J.E. & Wrzesniewski, A. *What Is Job Crafting and Why Does It Matter?* Michigan Ross School of Business. 2007. 0. https://www.researchgate.net/publication/266094577_What_is_Job_Crafting_and_Why_Does_It_Matter

182 *Bringing More Humanity To Recognition, Performance and Life at Work*. Globoforce. 2017. https://www.globoforce.com/wp-content/uploads/2017/10/WHRI_2017SurveyReportA.pdf

183 Guerrera, Francesco. *"Welch condemns share price focus."* Financial Times. March 12, 2009. https://www.ft.com/content/294ff1f2-0f27-11de-ba10-0000779fd2ac#axzz1eiLpL2PZ

184 Bower, Joseph L. & Paine, Lynn S. "The Error at the Heart of Corporate Leadership." *Harvard Business Review.* 95, no 3. June 2017. https://www.hbs.edu/faculty/Pages/item.aspx?num=52623

185 Denning, Steve. "Making Sense of Shareholder Value: 'The World's Dumbest Idea'." *Forbes.* July 17, 2017. https://www.forbes.com/sites/stevedenning/2017/07/17/making-sense-of-shareholder-value-the-worlds-dumbest-idea/#230844f92a7e

186 Hedges, Kristi. "5 Questions to Help Your Employees Find Their Inner Purpose". *Harvard Business Review.* August 17, 2017. https://hbr.org/2017/08/5-questions-to-help-your-employees-find-their-inner-purpose

187 "The Business Case For Purpose." *Harvard Business Review.* 2015. https://hbr.org/resources/pdfs/comm/ey/19392HBRReportEY.pdf

188 *Global Human Capital Trends 2015.* Deloitte University Press. 2015. https://www2.deloitte.com/content/dam/Deloitte/na/Documents/human-capital/na_DUP_GlobalHumanCapital-Trends2015.pdf

189 Tonin, Mirco. & Vlassopoulos, Michael. *Corporate Philanthropy and Productivity: Evidence from an Online Real Effort Experiment.* Center for Economic Studies & Ifo Institute. 2014. http://www.personal.soton.ac.uk/mv1u06/CP_WP.pdf

190 Marinova, S. V., Cao, X. & Park, H. "Constructive Organizational Values Climate and Organizational Citizenship Behaviours: a Configurational View." *Journal of Management.* 2018. https://doi.org/10.1177/0149206318755301

191 Chakraverty, Julie. "Company Vision and Values: Do They Still Matter?" *Forbes.* March 28, 2018. https://www.forbes.com/sites/voicesfromeurope/2018/03/28/company-vision-and-values-do-they-still-matter/#1857e2c3217f

192 *Aligned Companies Significantly Outperform Their Peers.* LSA Global. Accessed December 18, 2018. https://lsaglobal.com/insights/proprietary-methodology/lsa-3x-organizational-alignment-model/

193 Pulakos, E. D., Mueller-Hanson, R. A., O'Leary, R.S. & Meyrowitz, M.M. "Building a High Performance Culture: a Fresh Look at Performance Management." *SHRM Foundation's Effective Practice Guidelines Series.* 2012. https://www.shrm.org/foundation/our-work/initiatives/resources-from-past-initiatives/Documents/Building%20a%20High%20Performance%20Culture.pdf

194 Pulakos et al. "Building a High Performance Culture: a Fresh Look at Performance Management."

195 Pulakos et al. "Building a High Performance Culture: a Fresh Look at Performance Management."

196 *Effective Managers: Your Critical Link to Successful Strategy Execution.* Towers Watson. 2015. 5. https://bit.ly/2Gl3Lh4

197 Laguna, M., Alessandri, G. & Caprara, G. V. "Personal Goal Realization in Entrepreneurs: a Multilevel Analysis of the Role of Affect and Positive Orientation." *Applied Psychology.* Volume 65. 2016. https://onlinelibrary.wiley.com/doi/full/10.1111/apps.12061

198 Sagiv, Lilach & Schwartz, Shalom H. "Value priorities and subjective well-being: direct relations and congruity effects". *European Journal of Social Psychology.* 30(2). 2000. 177–198. http://citeseerx.ist.psu.edu/viewdoc/download?-doi=10.1.1.473.2329&rep=rep1&type=pdf

199 Alvesson, Mats & Spicer, André. "(Un)Conditional Surrender? Why Do Professionals Willingly Comply with Managerialism." *Journal of Organizational Change Management.* 2016. 29(1). http://openaccess.city.ac.uk/15605/

200 Brown, Brené. *Dare to Lead.* YouTube: CBS This Morning. October 10, 2018. https://www.youtube.com/watch?v=hEn-qV_M_Dm4

201 Comer, Debra R. & Sekerka, Leslie E. "Keep Calm and Carry On (Ethically): Durable Moral Courage in the Workplace." *Human Resource Management Review.* 28(2). 2018.116- 130. http://isiarticles.com/bundles/Article/pre/pdf/116035.pdf

ABOUT THE AUTHOR

Natasha Wallace

Natasha is founder and chief coach of Conscious Works, a leadership and personal development business specializing in performance and wellbeing. As a former HR director, Natasha left paid employment having reached burnout. It led her to recognize that people need to start working differently if they are to thrive. It means paying greater attention to our needs and the needs of others. The way to do this – to become more conscious and more aware, of ourselves and the people we lead. She set up her company to help leaders to create healthier workplaces where people could do a great job while taking care of their long-term health and wellbeing.

Natasha's main specialisms are in culture change, leadership development, and more recently, wellbeing. Having helped build an award-winning leadership development programme and through her work with Boards, Natasha has built a deep knowledge of what it takes to be a good leader and the pressures faced by modern day leaders.

It's through Conscious Leadership that Natasha now helps leaders and their teams to achieve sustainable results. Using coaching, leadership development and thought leadership, Natasha is getting leaders to revisit how they lead – themselves and others. Natasha is passionately dedicated to 'inspiring a well world of work' and is chair of the Engage for Success Wellbeing Thought and Action Group. She believes that through getting to know ourselves and our people better, we will create a better and more responsible world of work.